SURVIVAL

BOOKS BY MARGARET ATWOOD

FICTION

The Edible Woman (1969)

Surfacing (1972)

Lady Oracle (1976)

Dancing Girls (1977)

Life Before Man (1979)

Bodily Harm (1981)

Murder in the Dark (1983)

Bluebeard's Egg (1983)

The Handmaid's Tale (1985)

Cat's Eye (1988)

Wilderness Tips (1991)

Good Bones (1992)

The Robber Bride (1993)

Alias Grace (1996)

The Blind Assassin (2000)

Good Bones and Simple
Murders (2001)

Oryx and Crake (2003)

The Penelopiad (2005)

The Tent (2006)

Moral Disorder (2006)

The Year of the Flood (2009)

FOR CHILDREN

Up in the Tree (1978)

Anna's Pet [with Joyce
Barkhouse] (1980)

For the Birds (1990)

Princess Prunella and the Purple
Peanut (1995)

Rude Ramsay and the Roaring
Radishes (2003)

Bashful Bob and Doleful Dorinda
(2004)

Wandering Wenda and Widow
Wallop's Wunderground Washery
(2011)

NON-FICTION

Survival: A Thematic Guide to
Canadian Literature (1972)

Days of the Rebels 1815-1840 (1977)

Second Words (1982)

Strange Things: The Malevolent North
in Canadian Literature (1996)

Two Solicitudes: Conversations [with
Victor-Lévy Beaulieu] (1998)

Negotiating with the Dead: A Writer
on Writing (2002)

Moving Targets: Writing with Intent
1982–2004 (2004)

Curious Pursuits: Occasional Writing
(2005)

Writing with Intent: Essays, Reviews,
Personal Prose 1983–2005 (2005)

Payback: Debt and the Shadow Side
of Wealth (2008)

In Other Worlds: SF and the Human
Imagination (2011)

POETRY

Double Persephone (1961)

The Circle Game (1966)

The Animals in That Country (1968)

The Journals of Susanna
Moodie (1970)

Procedures for Underground (1970)

Power Politics (1971)

You Are Happy (1974)

Selected Poems (1976)

Two-Headed Poems (1978)

True Stories (1981)

Interlunar (1984)

Selected Poems II: Poems Selected and
New 1976-1986 (1986)

Morning in the Burned House (1995)

Eating Fire: Selected Poems 1965–
1995 (1998)

The Door (2007)

MARGARET ATWOOD

SURVIVAL

A THEMATIC GUIDE TO CANADIAN LITERATURE

A LIST

First published in 1972 by House of Anansi Press
First McClelland & Stewart edition 1996

This edition published in 2012 by
House of Anansi Press Inc.
110 Spadina Avenue, Suite 801
Toronto, ON, M5V 2K4
Tel. 416-363-4343
Fax 416-363-1017
www.houseofanansi.com

Distributed in Canada by
HarperCollins Canada Ltd.
1995 Markham Road
Scarborough, ON, M1B 5M8
Toll free tel. 1-800-387-0117

House of Anansi Press is committed to protecting our natural environment.
As part of our efforts, the interior of this book is printed on paper that contains 100% post-
consumer recycled fibres, is acid-free, and is processed chlorine-free.

"The Caverned Woman" from *The Boatman* by Jay Macpherson.
Permission of Oxford University Press, Canadian Branch.

"The Well-Travelled Roadway" from *Moving In Alone* by John Newlove.
Permission of the author.

All other quotations used represent excerpts only. For source of the complete work,
see book lists and "Sources of Epigraphs."

16 15 14 13 12   1 2 3 4 5

Library and Archives Canada Cataloguing in Publication

Atwood, Margaret, 1939–
Survival : a thematic guide to Canadian literature / Margaret Atwood.

Includes index.
Issued also in an electronic format.
ISBN 978-1-77089-252-1

1. Canadian literature — History and criticism. I. Title.

PS8061.A8 2012   C810.9   C2012-903363-4

Library of Congress Control Number: 2012939437

Cover design: Brian Morgan
Text design and typesetting: M&S, Toronto

Canada Council   Conseil des Arts
for the Arts   du Canada

ONTARIO ARTS COUNCIL
CONSEIL DES ARTS DE L'ONTARIO

*We acknowledge for their financial support of our publishing program
the Canada Council for the Arts, the Ontario Arts Council, and the Government of
Canada through the Canada Book Fund.*

Printed and bound in Canada

MIX
Paper from
responsible sources
FSC
www.fsc.org   FSC® C004071

ANCIENT FOREST ™
FRIENDLY

SURVIVAL: A Demi-Memoir
Margaret Atwood

Survival is a book about surviving. Specifically, it's a book about Canadian literature as I saw it forty-odd years ago. It's also about Canada itself as I saw it forty-odd years ago – because one of the axioms of this book is that a literature has something to do with the people who create it, and that the people who create it have something to do with where they live. One of the characteristics of Canada, then, was that not much attention was paid in it to Canadian literature. So the creators of Canadian literature – the writers – were working in a society that, historically and collectively, hadn't been much interested in them, except for the odd hit writer such as Ralph Connor, Robert W. Service, or A. M. Montgomery. Although there were a few academic studies at the time, there was no account for the general reader, and so infrequently was Canadian literature taught in schools and universities that many people assumed there wasn't any.

When *Survival* was published in 1972, it caused an uproar. This was something of a paradox: it's hard to imagine how a book about something thought either not to exist or not worthy to exist should have stirred things up as it did, and then – annoyingly – should have sold so many copies. But so it was. The raucous though unlikely success of *Survival* caused me to morph overnight from a lady poet with peculiar hair to the Wicked Witch of the North, accused of evil communism or bourgeois capitalistic sycophancy, though others greeted me as the long-awaited forger of the uncreated conscience of CanLit. I did not think I was either – I believed I was just writing a useful handbook to a little-known subject, a sort of early *Idiot's Guide*; but screens onto which images are projected seldom get a say as to the nature of those images, and neither did I.

However, notoriety generates sales, and the House of Anansi Press lived off the avails for many years. *Survival* arguably saw the House through the near-extinction bottleneck that threatened it in the mid-seventies. In fact, had there been no *Survival* then, you would probably not be reading *Survival* now.

If you published a book called *Survival* today, the reader would expect one of the following:

- A novelization of a popular TV series in which people strenuously eliminate one another.
- A memoir by a person who was molested in childhood, had alcoholic or otherwise dysfunctional parents, or escaped from a war zone, sinking passenger ship or natural disaster.
- A handbook for those who think the end of the world is near, and who want to know which roots are edible and how to roast a squirrel. The same handbook might be used for those interested merely in wilderness exploration.
- A fiction about how that very same end of the world is brought about by forces unknown, and/or climate change, and/or plague, natural or manmade, and/or widespread social meltdown caused by any number of things, and leading to warlords, atrocities, mutations, and cannibalism.

Survival stories – especially those about the end of the world – are popular at the moment: we're in a millennial mood, and not without reason: several of the end-of-the-world scenarios are already more than possible, and much head-scratching and bullet-dodging is being done by way of mitigation or denial.

But forty-five years ago, as the House of Anansi was taking shape, the imaginative landscape was quite different. If we feared annihilation, it was by atomic bomb: the Cuban missile crisis was a mere five years in the past. We were unaware of the fact that a spilled shipload or two of the Agent Orange being transported to Vietnam in massive quantities really could have wiped out humanity, by killing the oceanic algae that produce 80% of the world's oxygen.

The assassination of John F. Kennedy four years previously had drawn a line under Camelot idealism, but other idealisms were afloat: the Civil Rights Movement was in after-shock mode, the draft dodgers were flooding into Canada, psychedelic drugs were being hailed as a shortcut to nirvana, and the supposedly liberating sexual free-for-all unleashed by the Pill was gathering momentum. The women's movement had not yet unfurled, though there were mutterings. The mini-skirt was the fashion of the moment. Quite soon beards and love beads would sprout on hitherto buttoned-down men, and suburban housewives would try out lesbianism because, suddenly, they could, but that had not quite happened, such antics being still confined to a bohemian underworld that was not fully visible in the light of day.

Anansi was begun with the tools at hand, which did not include Xrox machines or instant transmission. There were no personal computers: typewriters and carbon paper were the norm. There were no answering machines. There were no cell phones. Long distance calls were expensive. If you wanted to communicate with someone elsewhere, you wrote a letter. There were no Canadian literary agents of the present kind. Canada thought of itself as a cultural backwater, and first-rate artistic items – books, films, music – were known to come from elsewhere. If you wanted to be serious about writing, back in, say, 1960, it was taken for granted that you had to leave the country.

But by 1967 it had become possible to stay. That was the year the House of Anansi was founded by Dennis Lee, poet, and Dave Godfrey, short-story writer. My own involvement with the House dates from the same year. Much to everyone's surprise, including mine, my first full-length collection, *The Circle Game* – published in 1966 by the poet-run Contact Press, with a cover made by me out of Letraset and red stick-on legal dots – had won the Governor General's Award for Poetry. But by the time of the award, the modest print run of 420 copies was gone.

I was standing in Hart House Theatre in Toronto during the intermission of an unremembered play when my old college friend Dennis Lee appeared out of nowhere. He said to me, "We're starting a publishing company, and we'd like to reprint *The Circle Game* as one of the first four books we're doing."

"How many copies were you thinking of?" I asked.

"Twenty-five hundred," he said. I thought he was mad. But as it turned out he was onto something, and that something was the growing idealism about the possibilities for Canadian writing among the young writers of that time. The first four Anansi poets each got a grant for $650 – Dennis somehow arranged it – and we rolled the money back into the company in return for shares. (I did not at that time know what a "share" was.) And so, with less than three thousand dollars but a lot of sweat equity, Anansi was born.

In Canada, most of the published younger writers were poets or short story writers, because it was hard to get such a long and expensive thing as a Canadian novel published then – we were told – without the participation of an American or British partner. So Anansi – like the other small publishers that appeared then – was at first a poets' press. Poetry readings had begun in the coffee houses of the early 60s and had spread to universities, though not yet to bookstores. Literary festivals were in the future. Still, there was a growing readership for Canadian writing.

There was a lot of interest in Canada itself that year. The focus was the world exhibition, Expo 67, held in Montreal over the summer and fall. This was a high point for Canada. After its excellent army record and its respected honest-broker position during World War II, Canada had lost the plot somewhat, despite the visionary rhetoric of John Diefenbaker, and Expo 67 was a chance to prove that Canada could get the plot back. Expo showed that Canadians, working together, could pull something off on the international stage, and do it not only with flair, but bilingually.

What a bright future shimmered ahead – illusory, like many things that shimmer. In four years Separatism would be upon us, the women's movement would be exploding like a water bomb, the West would be on the road to alienation and oil-fuelled power, and cultural regionalism would begin to resent what it would define as centralist cultural nationalism.

Over the same four years, between late 1967 and early 1972, I myself left Montreal, spent two years in Edmonton, published my first novel, wrote my second, published three books of poetry, spent a year in Europe, collaborated on a screenplay, moved back to Toronto, taught at York University, and developed the central argument at the core of *Survival*.

I kept up with Anansi through all of this by letter – advising on some of the books, editing a couple of others. We poets had the habit of dabbling in one another's manuscripts, just to be helpful. It was a very informal arrangement. The first time someone suggested to me that I should get paid for this kind of work I was taken aback. Would you charge for helping to push someone's car out of the snow?

While I was in Europe over 1970-71, Dennis wrote to ask me if I would join Anansi's board. I didn't know what a board was, but, perhaps foolishly, I joined it anyway. Then, upon my return to Canada, I found myself taking on most of the poetry list, and several works of fiction. (Anansi was doing fiction by then, having started with Graeme Gibson's runaway bestseller, *Five Legs*, which was copyedited by students at the shortly-to-become-notorious Rochdale College.)

Because of my board position, I participated in the regular handwringing and bloodletting angst sessions that substitute for board meetings among small publishers. How to pay the rent? (Not that the premises were palatial.) How to distribute? (We often sold our own books then, in high school gymnasiums, taking cash; credit cards were not yet widely deployed.) How to promote? (We crept around at night, stapling up posters on hoardings and telephone poles.) How to keep the price of books down? (Anansi was a pioneer of the split hardcover/trade paper run.) What to pay employees? (Never enough. Everyone was overworked and underpaid.)

As described in the Preface that follows this demi-memoir, *Survival* was initially proposed – and then composed at breakneck speed – as a stopgap solution to the rent problem: a grownup version of selling Girl Guide cookies. It would not have occurred to me to write such a book, otherwise.

What does *Survival* mean for today's readers, as they ask on radio shows? And – a separate question – what does it mean for me, its long-ago author? Is it a piece of nostalgia, like the photo of me in my Grade Twelve waltz-length formal – sweet, but a little embarrassing? The "Canada" it describes has changed a lot; in fact, it's changed even since I last wrote a Preface to *Survival*, back in 2003. For the most part, it hasn't gotten better.

Survival concludes by asking, "Have we survived?" We have, more or less, though the emotional space we call "Canada" is fraying at the edges and the institutions we thought of as being Canadian are being dismantled as quickly as the busy deconstruction crews of Ottawa elves can dismantle them. On the global stage – a stage where weird weather caused by climate change is in the spotlight – there's the sense that we're clinging on by our fingernails. Nature as Monster – a trope that preoccupied the writers of the nineteenth and early twentieth centuries, and that therefore features in *Survival* – is still with us, though we no longer fear that the monster will kill us. Now the situation is reversed: we will kill it, and in doing so seal our own doom, because you are what you breathe, and we and Nature were joined at the hip all along. In the forty years since *Survival*, the word "survival" has taken on several newer and more ominous levels of meaning. It isn't dreariness we fear now, as much as irreparable and self-inflicted disaster.

It's incredible that the House of Anansi has itself survived for forty-five years, and that it has gone beyond mere survival, and is now thriving. I hope it will persist for another forty-five years, and that Canada will persist as well – and that the reading of books will still take place then, and that readers will continue to find such reading an enjoyable and meaningful way to spend time. For if so, the human race will also have survived. And why should it not? Incredible things do happen.

Now for an upbeat ending. While re-reading this little book, I remembered that I had fun writing it – fun in the largest sense of the word. It was strenuous fun, like trying to roll a huge and unwieldy snowball uphill through a red-hot lava flow, but it was fun nevertheless; and fun is never to be sneezed at, especially in Canada.

Thank you, House of Anansi. You made me do it.

Introduction

In 1972, when I was thirty-two, I wrote and published the book you are now holding in your hands. It ignited a ferocious debate and became, as they say, a runaway best-seller, which was a shock to everyone, including me. Canadian writing, *interesting*? Among the bulk of readers at that time it was largely unknown, even in Canada, and among the cogno-scenti it was frequently treated as a dreary joke, an oxymoron, a big yawn, or the hole in a non-existent doughnut.

Survival was both an attempt to grapple with these attitudes and a symptom that they were changing. At the beginning of the 1960s, the usual sales of poetry books numbered in the hun-dreds, and any novel was doing well if it hit a thousand copies. But over that decade, things changed rapidly. After the wartime 1940s and the beige 1950s, Canada was showing a renewed interest in its own cultural doings. The Canada Council began supporting writers in earnest in 1965. In Québec, the Quiet Revolution had generated an outburst of literary activity; in the rest of Canada, many poets had emerged through coffee houses and public readings, more novelists and short-story writers were becoming known, and Expo 67, the Montreal world's fair, had created a fresh national self-confidence. Audiences had been building steadily, and by 1972 there was a critical mass of readers who wanted to hear more; and thus, through a combination of good luck, good timing, and good reviews, *Survival* became an "overnight publishing sensation," and I myself became an instant sacred monster. "Now you're a target," Farley Mowat said to me, "and they will shoot at you."

How prescient he was. Who could have suspected that this modest cultural artifact would have got so thoroughly up the noses of some of my elders and betters? If the book had sold the three thousand copies initially projected, nobody would have bothered their heads about it, but in the first year alone it sold ten times that number – huge for that time – and suddenly Canlit was everybody's business. The few dedicated academic souls who had cultivated this neglected pumpkin patch over the meagre years were affronted because a mere chit of a girl had appropriated a pumpkin they regarded as theirs, and those who had taken a firm stand on the non-existence of Canadian literature were affronted because I had pointed out that there was in fact a pumpkin *to* appropriate. After the first decade of this, I began to feel like the mechanical duck at the fun-fair shooting gallery, though nobody has won the oversized panda yet because I still seem to be quacking.

Over the years I've been accused of just about everything, from bourgeois superstition to communist rabble-rousing to not being Marshall McLuhan. Yet when I was writing this book – or rather when I was putting it together, for it drew on the work of my predecessors and the thoughts of my contemporaries, and was thus more an act of synthesis than one of authorship – I attached no particular importance to it. I was, after all, a poet and novelist, wasn't I? I did not consider myself a real critic – just a kind of bake-sale muffin lady, doing a little cottage-industry fundraising in a worthy cause.

The worthy cause was the House of Anansi Press, a small literary publisher formed in 1966 by writers Dennis Lee and David Godfrey – as many small houses were formed in those years – as a response to the dearth of publishing opportunities for new writing. Anansi was diverse in scope – Austin Clarke, Harold Sonny Ladoo, Roch Carrier, and Jacques Ferron were some of its authors – and the house had already made quite a few waves by 1971, when Dennis, an old college friend, button-hooked me onto its board. So there we were one grey November day, a tiny, intrepid, overworked, underpaid band, glumly contemplating the balance sheet, which showed an alarming amount of red ink. Publishing Rule Number One is that it's hard to keep small literary publishers solvent unless you have the equivalent of gardening books to support them, because even if by some fluke one of your authors does well, he or she will soon be courted by a larger publisher with more funds to offer. Small publishers are always opening gateways they can never walk through themselves.

To pay the bills, Anansi had begun a line of user-friendly self-help guides, which had done moderately well: *Law Law Law*, by Clayton Ruby and Paul Copeland, which set forth how to disinherit your relatives, avoid being bled dry by your estranged spouse, and so forth; and *VD*, one of the first venereal disease books, which explicated unwanted goo and warts, though AIDS was still a decade away. Such books, we'd found, sold more than first volumes of poetry.

Survival was conceived as another such easy-access book. As I'd travelled the country in the sixties, giving poetry readings and toting cardboard boxes of my own books to sell afterwards because often there was no bookstore, the absence of views on the subject was spectacular. The two questions I was asked most frequently by audience members were, "Is there any Canadian literature?" and, "Supposing there is, isn't it just a second-rate copy of *real* literature, which comes from England and the United States?" In Australia they called such attitudes the Cultural Cringe; in Canada they were termed the Colonial Mentality. In both – and in many smaller countries around the world – they were part of a tendency to believe that the Great Good Place was, culturally speaking, elsewhere.

In 1971-72, I happened to be doing a one-year teaching stint at York University, replacing a real professor who was on sabbatical. Canadian Literature formed, astonishingly, part of the course-load, so I'd had to come up with some easily grasped approaches to it – easily grasped by me as well as by my students, because I was, by training, a Victorianist, and had never formally studied Canadian literature. (Not surprising: when I was going through school, it wasn't taught much.) I discovered that previous thinkers on the subject, although pithy enough, had been few in number: there was not a wealth of existing lore. At the same time, there was now some interest in putting some already-existing Canadian novels into paperback: both McClelland & Stewart and Macmillan had initiated series of this kind. Without them it would have been difficult for me to teach my course, or indeed to write *Survival*.

Back to the Anansi meeting. "Hey, I know," I cried, in my Mickey Rooneyish way. "Let's do a *VD* of Canadian Literature!" What I meant, I explained, was a handbook for the average reader – for all those people I'd met on my tours who'd wanted to learn more but didn't know where to start. This book would not be for academics. It would have no footnotes, and would not employ the phrase *on the other hand*, or at least not much. It would also contain an appendix – some lists of other books, and music too, that people could actually go into a bookstore and *buy*. This was a fairly revolutionary concept, because the Canlit of the past was mostly out of print, and that of the present was kept well hidden at the back of the store, in among the Beautiful Canadiana fall foliage calendars.

We now take it for granted that Canadian literature is an acknowledged category, but this proposition was not always self-evident. To have any excuse for being, the kind of book I had in mind would have to prove several points. First, that, yes, there was a Canadian literature – such a thing did indeed exist. (This turned out to be a radical proposition, and was disputed by many when the book appeared.) Second, that this body of work was not just a feeble version of English or American, or, in the case of francophone books, of French literature, but that it had different preoccupations, which were specific to its own history and geopolitics. This too was a radical proposition, although common sense ought to have indicated that it was merely common sense: If you were a rocky, watery northern country, cool in climate, large in geographical expanse, small but diverse in population, and with a huge aggressive neighbour to the south, why wouldn't you have concerns that varied from those of the huge aggressive neighbour? Or indeed from those of the crowded, history-packed, tight little island, recently but no longer an imperial power, that had once ruled the waves? You'd think they'd be different, wouldn't you? To justify the teaching of Canadian literature as such, here and now, thirty-four years later, you'd still have to start from the same axioms: i) it exists, and ii) it's distinct.

Back to the Anansi meeting, again. The board agreed that there would be no harm in our trying, though Canlit might not exert the fascination of – say – a venereal wart. Over the next four or five months, I wrote away at the book, and as I finished each section Dennis Lee edited it, and under Dennis's blue pencil the book grew from the proposed hundred-page handbook to a length of almost 250 pages. It also took on a more coherent shape and direction. Several other people at Anansi also worked hard on this group project, researching various resources, checking facts, giving feedback. It was a collective effort, more like producing a college revue than writing a book.

The book's subtitle – *A Thematic Guide to Canadian Literature* – meant that we were aiming not at an all-inclusive cross-indexed survey such as was provided in 1997 by the 1,199-page *Oxford Companion to Canadian Literature*, nor at a series of studies of this author or that, nor at a collection of New-critical close readings or *explications du texte*. We were doing the sort of thing that art historian Nicholas Pevsner had done in *The Englishness of English Art*, or that the American literary critic Leslie Fiedler was doing in his examinations of American literature: the identification of a series of characteristics and leitmotifs, and a comparison of the varying treatments of them in different national and cultural environments. I was familiar with this approach, having studied American literature at the Harvard Graduate School with Perry Miller.

For example: Money as a sign of divine grace or providence is present in the American tradition from the Puritans through Benjamin Franklin through *Moby-Dick* through Henry James through *The Great Gatsby*. The theme is treated now seriously, now cynically, now tragically, now ironically, just as a leitmotif in a symphony may be played in different keys and in different tempos. It varies as time unrolls and circumstances change, of course: the eighteenth century of Franklin is not the twentieth century of Scott Fitzgerald. Yet the leitmotif persists as a dominating concern – a persistent cultural obsession, if you like.

The persistent cultural obsession of Canadian literature, said *Survival* in 1972, was survival. In actual life, and in both the anglophone and the francophone sectors, this concern was often enough a factor of the weather, as when the ice storm cuts off the electrical power. *La survivance* had long been an overt theme in Québec political life, manifesting itself in the latter half of the twentieth century as anxiety about the survival of French. In the rest of Canada, the anxiety was more free-floating, and ranged from the fear of being squashed by trees or destroyed by icebergs to the feeling of being stifled by the society around you.

Survival, therefore, began with this dominant note. It then postulated a number of other motifs in Canadian literature – motifs that either did not exist at all in one of the literatures chosen for comparison (for instance, there are almost no "Indians" in English novels), or which did exist but were not handled in the same way. The Canadian "immigrant story," from fleeing Loyalists to Scots kicked off their land to starving Irish to Latvians emigrating after the Second World War to the economic refugees that came later, tends to be very different when told in the United States: none of their stories is likely to say that the immigrants were really trying to get into Canada but ended up in the United States *faute de mieux*. When I was writing *Survival*, Canada had rarely been seen as the promised land, except by escaped slaves travelling the Underground Railroad. That it is now picked as the destination of choice by many immigrants is a measure of how much things have changed.

The pre-1972 tradition identified in *Survival* was not a bundle of uplifting Pollyanna cheer: quite the reverse. Canlit, at least up until 1970, was on balance a somewhat dour concoction. Some critics who couldn't read very well thought I was somehow *advocating* this state of affairs. *Au contraire*: if the book has an attitude, it's more like *you are here, you really do exist, and this is where, so pull up your socks and quit whining.* As Alice Munro says, "Do what you want and live with the consequences." Or as *Survival* itself said in its last chapter, "Having bleak ground under your feet is better than having no ground at all . . . a tradition doesn't necessarily exist to bury you: it can also be used as material for new departures."

Many things have happened in the thirty-four years since *Survival* was first published. In politics, the Québec question and the loss of national control and increased U.S. domination brought about by the 1989 Free Trade Agreement have become, not the tentative warning notes they were in *Survival*, but everyday realities. Canada's well-known failure to embrace a single "identity" of the yodelling or Beefeater variety has come to seem less like a failure than a deliberate and rather brave refusal: it's interesting to remember that during the flag debate under Lester Pearson it was seriously proposed by some that Canada adopt no flag at all, thus breaking new ground. In literary criticism, Regionalism, Feminism, Deconstructionism, Political Correctness, Appropriation of Voice, and Identity Politics have all swept across the scene, leaving their traces. Many new writers from diverse ethnic backgrounds have added their stories. The chapter on Women, if written now, would be quite different; so would the one on the Failed Artist, appropriate for its time because very few artists succeeded then, but no longer the only story possible. So would the one called First Peoples: in 1972, few native people – with the quasi-exception of Pauline Johnson – had been writers, and those few had written only biographies. Now there are poets, playwrights, novelists, and short-story writers.

Technologies have altered the way we communicate; the scorned tree-huggers of yesteryear have become the respected alternate-energy gurus of today; Nature the Monster, though it can still kill you, is more likely to be seen as Nature the Threatened, as predicted in the original *Survival*. The former Canadian-identity question, "Where is here?" has been replaced by "Who are we?" In academia, *discourse* and *text* are the new words for *debate* and *book*. *Problematize* has become a verb, and *postmodern* – once a cutting-edge adjective – has faded away in its turn.

Survival, the book, seemed quainter and more out of date as these various years went by, and – incidentally – as some of its wishes were granted and some of its predictions realized. Yet its central concerns remain with us, and must still be confronted. Are we really that different from anybody else? If so, how? And is that *how* something worth preserving?

People often ask me what I would change about *Survival* if I were writing it today. I used to fool around with some possible additions – a chapter on Canadian war novels, one on Canadian humour, one on genre writing such as the crime novel. I should certainly have paid more attention to Morley Callaghan, and Hugh MacLennan, and – yes – Mazo de la Roche. And him, and him, and her, and her. However, the real answer is that I wouldn't write *Survival* today, because I wouldn't need to. The thing I set out to prove has been proven beyond a doubt: few would seriously argue, any more, that there is no Canadian literature. The other answer is that I wouldn't be able to write it, not only because of my own hardening brain, but because the quantity, range, and diversity of books now published would defeat any such effort. Mordecai Richler's well-known jest, "world-famous in Canada," has ceased to be such a laugh – many Canadian writers are now world-famous, period.

The erstwhile molehill of Canlit has grown to a mountain. The fully bilingual Institute for Canadian Studies at the University of Ottawa lists some 279 Canadian Studies centres located in other countries, including 20 in France, 65 in the United States, 16 in Germany, and 22 in India. Canadian writers regularly achieve foreign publication, win major international prizes, and sign movie deals. For a country with the population of Illinois or Mexico City, we've done more than well – we've done spectacularly. The success of Canadian writers, both at home and around the world, has been one of the biggest surprises for those of us who began in the 1950s and 1960s.

But this is Canada, land of contrasts. Indeed it is Canada, land of rugs: no sooner has a rug been placed beneath the nation's artistic feet than it is pulled out. It's almost as if the old mingy attitudes were still with us: do well at something, and the small town punishes you for standing out. Nor does there seem to be a comprehension – at least in government-policy circles – of the fact that publishing and book distribution and reading and writing are connected to one another. Canada is an odd country: patriotism has always been regarded with some suspicion in it, because – as in any satrapy – getting too uppity about yourself might offend the imperial centre and thus be bad for business.

But that's another story. Here, instead, is the original *Survival*, shorn of its out-of-date appendices. It's a book of its own time and place: it could hardly have appeared before, or after, or anywhere else. It had a specific agenda – to raise debate around a subject its author considered crucial – and at that it succeeded, although its author has had to dodge a few brickbats since. It also had a specific genesis: a ways and means discussion at a small literary publishing house in Toronto. How to keep such an enterprise afloat?

One could also ask, Why keep it afloat? Why give your blood? The general answer is the same as it always was: a country needs to hear its own voices, if it is to become or to remain an aware society and a functioning democracy. The answer more specific to literature is also the same now: small publishers are the doors through which future writers most often pass. Close them, and you will still have the big fish, for a while. But as every fisherman knows, when all the fish in the lake are big you're in trouble, because there are no small but growing ones to take their places.

Most Canadian literary publishers in these hard times are still asking themselves the original *Survival* question. And the country asks it too. Every year or so there's a major magazine feature called something like: *Canada: Gone in Twenty Years?* Or, *Should Canada Join the States?* How Canadian of us, to ponder our own potential disappearance with such gloomy pleasure. At the same time, polls indicate that our consciousness of our *Canadianness* – would that word even have been used in 1972? – has increased, and that our attitudes continue to diverge from those of the folks south of us. Such books as *Mondo Canuck* and Douglas Coupland's *Souvenir of Canada* testify to our continuing interest in our own field markings.

The original *Survival* question was: *Have we survived?*

It was a good place to end in 1972, and it's a good place now.

Margaret Atwood
Toronto
October 2003

A different version of this introduction first appeared in *Maclean's* (Vol. 112, Issue 26; July 1, 1999).

SURVIVAL: THE 1972 ORIGINAL

For Jay Macpherson,
Northrop Frye, D. G. Jones,
James Reaney, Eli Mandel
and Dennis Lee

We shall unjoint our limbs
   and set them in a row for listing
To see what is lacking
To find the joint that is out of joint
For it is unthinkable to sit
   quietly accepting
   the body of this death. . . .

– Saint-Denys-Garneau,
"The Body of This Death"

Telling it in plain words
Makes me see how I feared the wrong thing.

– Margaret Avison,
"The Agnes Cleves Papers"

Tributes

This book received help in the form of suggestions and criticism from so many directions that it is practically a community effort. In particular I should like to thank James Foley and A. B. Hodgetts, who liked the idea; Matt Cohen for his helpful insights and the notion of "displacement"; James Polk, who thought first about animal victims; Michael Charters, the title of whose novel, *Victor/Victim*, provided a very useful phrase; and Jay Macpherson, Scott Symons, Rick Salutin, Charles Pachter, Shirley Gibson, John Rich, Robin Mathews and Dave Godfrey, for aid both spiritual and practical. Also Beth Appledoorn of the Longhouse Bookstore in Toronto, Harald Bohne of the University of Toronto Press, Carol Vine of the SCM Bookstore in Toronto, and Skye Morrison of Sheridan College. Also Jack Warwick and Mary Lou Piggott, who mushed through sleet and storm to hear some of these ideas in earlier forms. And, especially, Ann Wall, who compiled the material for the *Resources* section, Gary Hophan who did the Index, and the invaluable Dennis Lee, who helped create order from chaos.

The accuracies and fine points in this book were for the most part contributed by others; the sloppy generalizations are my own.

– M. A., July 1972.

TABLE OF CONTENTS

Preface

He doesn't want to talk about Canada. . . . There you have the Canadian dilemma in a sentence. Nobody wants to talk about Canada, not even us Canadians. You're right, Paddy. Canada is a bore.

– Brian Moore,
The Luck of Ginger Coffey

Searchers for a Canadian identity have failed to realize that you can only have an identification with something you can see or recognize. You need, if nothing else, an image in a mirror. No other country cares enough about us to give us back an image of ourselves that we can even resent. And apparently we can't do it for ourselves, because so far our attempts to do so have resembled those of the three blind men trying to describe the elephant. Some of the descriptions have been worth something, but what they add up to is fragmented, indecipherable. With what are we to identify ourselves?

– Germaine Warkentin,
"An Image In a Mirror"

It is true that no particularism can adequately incarnate the good. But is it not also true that only through some particular roots, however partial, can human beings first grasp what is good and it is the juice of such roots which for most men sustain their partaking in a more universal good?

– George Grant,
Technology and Empire

It seems to me that Canadian sensibility has been profoundly disturbed, not so much by our famous problem of identity, important as that is, as by a series of paradoxes in what confronts that identity. It is less perplexed by the question "Who am I?" than by some such riddle as "Where is here?"

– Northrop Frye,
The Bush Garden

With the maps lost, the voyages
Cancelled by legislation years ago,
This is become a territory without a name.

– Margaret Avison,
"Not the Sweet Cicely of Gerardes Herball"

What, Why, and Where Is Here?

When I started to write this book I intended to produce a short, easy-to-use guide to Canadian literature, largely for the benefit of students and of those teachers in high schools, community colleges and universities who suddenly find themselves teaching a subject they have never studied: "Canlit." Through my own struggles with the same problem I knew there was a considerable amount of material already available, but it consisted primarily of all-inclusive historical surveys, individual biographies, or in-depth academic studies which discuss works often out of print. In Canada there are many authors and many books, but few obvious classics; as a result, those compiling sources or distributing information tend to fall back on long lists of writers and book-titles, among which the prospective reader or teacher must scrabble around and choose as best he may. But the inevitable question will be raised, sooner or later, in one or another of its forms: "Why are we studying *him* (instead of Faulkner)?" "Why do we have to read *this* (instead of Hermann Hesse)?" Or, in its true shape, "What's Canadian about Canadian literature, and why should we be bothered?"

Before I attempt an answer to this question I should say what this book is not.

- It is not an exhaustive, extensive or all-inclusive treatise on Canadian literature. Several of these exist already and are listed at the end of this Preface; they *are* all-inclusive, and therefore fairly long. Because this book is short it must leave out much writing which is important and good. I have not tried to make my citations add up to a "balanced" overview of what's been written in Canada, and there are a couple of reasons for this.

    The first is that I'm a writer rather than an academic or an expert, and I've taken my examples where I've found them, not through study or research but in the course of my own reading. The second is that this is a book of patterns, not of authors or individual works; the point is not to divide up citations on an equal-space basis but to see as clearly as possible those patterns of theme, image and attitude which hold our literature together. If the patterns are really there, variations of them will be found in the work of writers I may have overlooked, excluded because there was something that exemplified the pattern more obviously, or never even heard of. A reader who finds this approach worthwhile won't stop with the examples I give; they are merely a starting-point.

- It is not a treatment of historical development. That is, it does not begin with the first books ever written in Canada and work its way up to the present. It's more helpful to start with a recognition of the situation you find yourself in, whatever it may be, and then look back to see how you got there. Thus you won't find much here about the Confederation Poets or about early Canadian fur-trader journals. I don't deny the importance of these but I don't think they are the best way in. Most though not all of my examples are drawn from the twentieth century, and many from the last few decades.

- It is not evaluative. I try to refrain from handing out merit badges, and no admiring reader should feel elated or put down because his favourite author is or isn't included. Though I try not to include any books I myself find tedious, it isn't "good writing" or "good style" or "literary excellence" I'm talking about here.

- It is not biographical. You'll find nothing at all here about the doubtless fascinating private lives of the authors concerned. I've treated the books as though they were

4

written by Canada, a fiction I hope you'll go along with
temporarily. It's a fiction that corrects an imbalance: we
all know that authors are private people, but until recently
our authors were treated *only* as private people. Authors
are also transmitters of their culture.

- It is not particularly original. Many of the ideas that
  inform it have been floating around, diffused in scholarly
  journals and private conversations, for a number of years;
  some of the places you can find them are also listed at the
  end of the Preface. My book stands in relation to them as
  a vitamin pill to a gourmet meal; it has the virtue of being
  cheaper to acquire and faster to swallow, but it misses out
  on a lot of overtones and refinements. It bypasses, too,
  many ripe nits that could well be picked; but I leave the
  plucking of these to others who perhaps find such pursuits
  more enjoyable.

Then, you may ask, if my book does not survey, evaluate,
provide histories or biographies or offer original and brilliant
insights, what does it do? It attempts one simple thing. It outlines a number of key patterns which I hope will function like
the field markings in bird-books: they will help you distinguish
this species from all others, Canadian literature from the other
literatures with which it is often compared or confused. Each
key pattern must occur often enough in Canadian literature
as a whole to make it significant. These key patterns, taken
together, constitute the shape of Canadian literature insofar as
it is *Canadian* literature, and that shape is also a reflection of a
national habit of mind.

As a collection of patterns the book may be used in various
ways. The patterns may be held up against books not mentioned here, to see if they apply. Or the entire sequence of

patterns may be covered by reading, for instance, one book from each chapter. Or one or two patterns may be studied in depth. (For teachers who live in areas where four-letter words still cause restiveness, I recommend Chapter Three; it's about animals, who fortunately speak neither English nor French, sacred or profane.) Another hint: read the quotations at the beginnings of the chapters. They've been chosen with care.

This, then, is a description of what I intended to write: something that would make Canadian literature, as *Canadian* literature – not just literature that happened to be written in Canada – accessible to people other than scholars and specialists, and that would do it with simplicity and practicability. But I find that what I've written is something more, a cross between a personal statement, which most books are, and a political manifesto, which most books also are, if only by default. Until recently, reading Canadian literature has been for me and for everyone else who did it a personal interest, since it was not taught, required or even mentioned (except with derision) in the public sphere. Like many of those who encountered it before, say, 1965, my involvement with it has been as a writer, not as a student or teacher, and several though by no means all of the patterns I've found myself dealing with here were first brought to my attention by my own work. Also by my surprise at finding the concerns of that work shared by writers with whom – I found myself concluding – I seemed to participate in a cultural community that had never been defined for me. I don't talk much about my work in this book because I happen to believe that an author is always his own trickiest critic. However, I approach many of the patterns, and the problems connected with them, from the writer's point of view; which is perhaps the best one, since that's how the writers themselves approach them. The answer to the question, "What is there to read about in this country?" is really also an answer to the question, "What is there to write about in this country?"

Writing Canadian literature has been historically a very private act, one from which even an audience was excluded, since for a lot of the time there was no audience. Teaching it, however, is a political act. If done badly it can make people even more bored with their country than they already are; if done well, it may suggest to them *why* they have been taught to be bored with their country, and whose interests that boredom serves.

But back to my original question. The first part of that question, "What's Canadian about Canadian literature," is answered, I hope, by the rest of this book. The second part, "Why should we be bothered," shouldn't have to be answered at all because, in any self-respecting nation, it would never even be asked. But that's one of the problems: Canada *isn't* a self-respecting nation and the question does get asked. Therefore.

The answers you get from literature depend on the questions you pose. If you ask, "Why do writers write?" the answer will be psychological or biographical. If you ask, "*How* do they write?" you may get an answer something like "With a pencil" or "With pain," or you may get an answer that talks about how the books are put together, an answer that treats the book as a self-contained verbal pattern and talks about style or form. These are entirely legitimate questions; but the one I'm concerned with here is "What do writers write about?"

The character Stephen Dedalus in James Joyce's *Portrait of the Artist as a Young Man* looks at the flyleaf of his geography book and finds a list he has written there:

Stephen Dedalus
Class of Elements
Clongowes Wood College
Sallins
County Kildare
Ireland
Europe
The World
The Universe

That's a fairly inclusive list of everything it is possible for a human being to write about and therefore to read about. It begins with the personal, continues through the social or cultural or national and ends with "The Universe," the universal. Any piece of fiction or poetry may contain elements of all three areas, though the ratio may vary: a love lyric is more likely to be personal or universal than it is to be national, a novel may be about a family or about a man's life as a politician, and so forth. The tendency in Canada, at least in high school and university teaching, has been to emphasize the personal and the universal but to skip the national or cultural. This is like trying to teach human anatomy by looking only at the head and the feet. That's one reason for reading Canadian literature then; it gives you a more complete idea of how any literature is made: it's made by people living in a particular space at a particular time, and you can recognize that more easily if the space and the time are your own. If you read only the work of dead foreigners you will certainly reinforce the notion that literature can be written only by dead foreigners.

But there's another reason that has to do not with the reader as student of literature but with the reader as citizen. A piece of art, as well as being a creation to be enjoyed, can also be (as

Germaine Warkentin suggests) a mirror. The reader looks at the mirror and sees not the writer but himself; and behind his own image in the foreground, a reflection of the world he lives in. If a country or a culture lacks such mirrors it has no way of knowing what it looks like; it must travel blind. If, as has long been the case in this country, the viewer is given a mirror that reflects not him but someone else, and told at the same time that the reflection he sees is himself, he will get a very distorted idea of what he is really like. He will also get a distorted idea of what other people are like: it's hard to find out who anyone else is until you have found out who *you* are. Self-knowledge, of course, can be painful, and the extent to which Canadian literature has been neglected in its home territory suggests, among other things, a fear on the part of Canadians of knowing who they are; while the large number of mirror and reflection images contained within that literature suggest a society engaged in a vain search for an image, a reflection that will answer it, like A. M. Klein's mad poet who "stares at a mirror all day long, as if / to recognize himself."

There are, of course, reflections of us to be found in places other than Canadian literature. There's the placid, jolly, woodcutting and woodchuck-eating "Canadian" in Thoreau's *Walden*; there's Edmund Wilson saying "In my youth, of the early nineteen-hundreds, we tended to imagine Canada as a kind of vast hunting preserve convenient to the United States." (Right on, Edmund.) In Malcolm Lowry's *Under the Volcano*, Canada is the protagonist's cool fantasy escape-land; if he can only make it there from steamy Mexico, everything will be all right. There's Shreve, the pinkish-grey Canadian roommate of Faulkner's Quentin in *Absalom, Absalom!* who is healthy, does exercises and plays Wedding Guest to Quentin's Ancient Mariner. And, for fun, there's the Canadian man who carries off the protagonist's girlfriend in Radclyffe Hall's *The Well of Loneliness*, the first Lesbian novel; he's muscular, competent, faceless and *heterosexual*. That's more or less the range of Canada as viewed by "international" literature: a place you escape to from "civilization," an unspoiled, uncorrupted place imagined as empty or thought of as populated by happy archaic peasants or YMCA instructors, quaint or dull or both. Watching made-in-Canada beer ads and tourist literature often gives you the uneasy feeling that the perpetrators are basing their images on these kinds of reflections because that's what everyone, inside and out, wants to believe. But Canadian literature itself tells a very different story.

To say that you must read your own literature to know who you are, to avoid being a sort of cultural moron, is not the same as saying that you should read nothing else, though the "internationalist" or Canada Last opponents of this notion sometimes think it is. A reader cannot live by Canlit alone, and it is a disservice to Canlit to try it. If a man from outer space were to be dropped on an island and supplied with all of Canadian literature and nothing else, he would be rendered completely incapable of deducing anything meaningful about *Canadian* literature because he would have nothing to compare it with; he would take it to be human literature *in toto*. The study of Canadian literature ought to be comparative, as should the study of any literature; it is by contrast that distinctive patterns show up most strongly. To know ourselves, we must know our own literature; to know ourselves accurately, we need to know it as part of literature as a whole.

But in Canada, as Frye suggests, the answer to the question "Who am I?" is at least partly the same as the answer to another question: "Where is here?" "Who am I?" is a question appropriate in countries where the environment, the "here," is already well-defined, so well-defined in fact that it may threaten to overwhelm the individual. In societies where everyone and everything has its place a person may have to struggle to separate himself from his social background, in order to keep from being just a function of the structure.

"Where is here?" is a different kind of question. It is what a man asks when he finds himself in unknown territory, and it implies several other questions. Where is this place in relation to other places? How do I find my way around in it? If the man is really lost he may also wonder how he got "here" to begin with, hoping he may be able to find the right path or possibly the way out by retracing his steps. If he is unable to do this he will have to take stock of what "here" has to offer in the way of support for human life and decide how he should go about remaining alive. Whether he survives or not will depend partly on what "here" really contains – whether it is too hot, too cold, too wet or too dry for him – and partly on his own desires and skills – whether he can utilize the resources available, adapt to what he can't change, and keep from going crazy. There may be other people "here" already, natives who are co-operative, indifferent or hostile. There may be animals, to be tamed, killed and eaten, or avoided. If, however, there is too large a gap between our hero's expectations and his environment he may develop culture shock or commit suicide.

There's a good moment in Carol Bolt's play *Buffalo Jump*: a high-school teacher in the thirties makes his students recite the names of all the wives of Henry the Eighth while a protest march is going past the window. He tells them they aren't in school to watch parades, which just about sums up the approach to Canadian history and culture that prevailed for many decades: history and culture were things that took place elsewhere, and if you saw them just outside the window you weren't supposed to look.

The wives of Henry the Eighth may be taken as standing for the deluge of values and artefacts flowing in from outside, from "there"; America, England or France. The values and artefacts – and they could as easily be symbolized by comic books, portraits of the Queen, The Ed Sullivan Show or marches on Ottawa (!) to stop the war in Vietnam – imply that "there" is always more important than "here" or that "here" is just another, inferior, version of "there"; they render invisible the values and artefacts that actually exist "here," so that people can look at a thing without really seeing it, or look at it and mistake it for something else. A person who is "here" but would rather be somewhere else is an exile or a prisoner; a person who is "here" but *thinks* he is somewhere else is insane.

But when you are here and don't know where you are because you've misplaced your landmarks or bearings, then you need not be an exile or a madman: you are simply lost. Which returns us to our image of the man in an unknown territory. Canada is an unknown territory for the people who live in it, and I'm not talking about the fact that you may not have taken a trip to the Arctic or to Newfoundland, you may not have explored – as the travel folders have it – This Great Land of Ours. I'm talking about Canada as a state of mind, as the space you inhabit not just with your body but with your head. It's that kind of space in which we find ourselves lost.

What a lost person needs is a map of the territory, with his own position marked on it so he can see where he is in relation to everything else. Literature is not only a mirror; it is also a map, a geography of the mind. Our literature is one such map, if we can learn to read it as *our* literature, as the product of who and where we have been. We need such a map desperately, we need to know about here, because here is where we live. For the members of a country or a culture, shared knowledge of their place, their here, is not a luxury but a necessity. Without that knowledge we will not survive.

How to Use This Book

One of the ideas behind *Survival* was to make a coherent overview of Canadian literature readily accessible to as many people as possible. To this end the book includes a number of lists which should help you to put your finger immediately on things you want. The lists break down as follows:

At the end of each chapter there is:
A SHORT LIST, for the convenience of teachers and readers pressed for time. It rarely includes more than four books. It lists author, title, publisher and price; and one of the criteria for inclusion is that the book must be available in paperback. Prices quoted are retail bookstore prices; remember that most publishers give educational discounts.

A LONG LIST, which includes everything mentioned in the chapter. It lists title, author and publisher, and lets you know whether the book is out of print. (Even if it is, libraries may well have it.)

At the end of the book there is:
Sources of Epigraphs: this section lists, by chapter, where you can find the complete poems or works from which the quotations at the beginning of each chapter are taken. (Prose quotes list page number; poem quotes do not, as poems are easily located in Table of Contents.)

An **Author Index.**

ABBREVIATIONS FOR FREQUENTLY-MENTIONED PUBLISHERS:

AN: House of Anansi Press.
M&S: McClelland & Stewart.
NCL: New Canadian Library, McClelland & Stewart.
N: New Press.
OUP: Oxford University Press
R: Ryerson, now McGraw-Hill-Ryerson.
UTP: University of Toronto Press.

Other publishers are mentioned by full name.

OP: Out of print.

ABBREVIATIONS FOR FREQUENTLY-MENTIONED ANTHOLOGIES:

G&B: Gary Geddes and Phyllis Bruce, eds., *Fifteen Canadian Poets*; OUP, $3.95.
ML: Eli Mandel, ed., *Poets of Contemporary Canada*; NCL, $2.95.
PMC: Milton Wilson, ed., *Poets of Mid-Century*; NCL, $2.35.
W1:   Robert Weaver, ed., *Canadian Short Stories*; OUP, $1.95.
W2:   Robert Weaver, ed., *Canadian Short Stories*, Second Series; OUP, $2.95.

I

SURVIVAL

When your love is a sour taste
in the mouth, become a matter
for apologies, survive.
. . .
When your face goes flat in
the silvered mirror, endure;
endure, if you can, and survive.

– John Newlove,
"If You Can"

It is the time of death
and the fear of never
having lived at all
crazes the young
when pigs that escaped slaughter
eat dozens of fermented
apples and charge drunken thru
empty woods
and huntsmen somewhere else
are learning the trade

– Al Purdy,
"Autumn"

. . . Lionel was lonely. The months passed. Lionel was lonely.
The months passed. They were too close to one another. Secretly
Lionel wanted to climb a tree and watch his own funeral. He
did not know this. . . .

– Russell Marois,
The Telephone Pole

I'm starting to feel sentimental
only when at home

in my sixty-dollar-a-month slum,
or to feel like a Canadian

only when kissing someone else's bum.

– *John Newlove,*
"Like a Canadian"

To find words for what we suffer,
To enjoy what we must suffer –
Not to be dumb beasts. . . .
    . . . .
    . . . We shall survive
And we shall walk

Somehow into summer. . . .

– *D. G. Jones,*
"Beating the Bushes: Christmas 1963"

I started reading Canadian literature when I was young, though I didn't know it was that; in fact I wasn't aware that I lived in a country with any distinct existence of its own. At school we were being taught to sing "Rule, Britannia" and to draw the Union Jack; after hours we read stacks of Captain Marvel, Plastic Man and Batman comic books, an activity delightfully enhanced by the disapproval of our elders. However, someone had given us Charles G. D. Roberts' *Kings in Exile* for Christmas, and I snivelled my way quickly through these heart-wrenching stories of animals caged, trapped and tormented. That was followed by Ernest Thompson Seton's *Wild Animals I Have Known*, if anything more upsetting because the animals were more actual – they lived in forests, not circuses – and their deaths more mundane: the deaths, not of tigers, but of rabbits.

No one called these stories Canadian literature, and I wouldn't have paid any attention if they had; as far as I was concerned they were just something else to read, along with Walter Scott, Edgar Allan Poe and Donald Duck. I wasn't discriminating in my reading, and I'm still not. I read then primarily to be entertained, as I do now. And I'm not saying that apologetically: I feel that if you remove the initial gut response from reading – the delight or excitement or simply the enjoyment of being told a story – and try to concentrate on the meaning or the shape or the "message" first, you might as well give up, it's too much like all work and no play.

But then as now there were different levels of entertainment. I read the backs of Shredded Wheat boxes as an idle pastime, Captain Marvel and Walter Scott as fantasy escape – I knew, even then, that wherever I lived it wasn't *there*, since I'd never seen a castle and the Popsicle Pete prizes advertised on the comic book covers either weren't available in Canada, or cost more – and Seton and Roberts as, believe it or not, something closer to real life. I *had* seen animals, quite a few of them; a dying porcupine was more real to me than a knight in armour or Clark Kent's Metropolis. Old mossy dungeons and Kryptonite were hard to come by where I lived, though I was quite willing to believe they existed somewhere else; but the materials for Seton's stick-and-stone artefacts and live-off-the-land recipes in *Wildwood Wisdom* were readily available, and we could make them quite easily, which we did. Most of the recipes were somewhat inedible, as you'll see if you try Cat-tail Root Stew or Pollen Pancakes, but the raw ingredients can be collected around any Canadian summer cottage.

However, it wasn't just the content of these books that felt more real to me; it was their shapes, their patterns. The animal stories were about the struggle to survive, and Seton's practical handbook was in fact a survival manual: it laid much stress on the dangers of getting lost, eating the wrong root or berry, or angering a moose in season. Though it was full of helpful hints, the world it depicted was one riddled with pitfalls, just as the animal stories were thickly strewn with traps and snares. In this world, no Superman would come swooping out of the sky at the last minute to rescue you from the catastrophe; no rider would arrive post-haste with a pardon from the King. The main thing was to avoid dying, and only by a mixture of cunning, experience and narrow escapes could the animal – or the human relying on his own resources – manage that. And, in the animal stories at any rate, there were no final happy endings or ultimate solutions; if the animal happened to escape from the particular crisis in the story, you knew there would be another one later on from which it wouldn't escape.

I wasn't making these analytical judgments at the time, of course. I was just learning what to expect: in comic books and things like *Alice in Wonderland* or Conan Doyle's *The Lost*

World, you got rescued or you returned from the world of dangers to a cozy safe domestic one; in Seton and Roberts, because the world of dangers was *the same* as the real world, you didn't. But when in high school I encountered – again as a Christmas present – something labelled more explicitly as Canadian Literature, the Robert Weaver and Helen James anthology, *Canadian Short Stories*, I wasn't surprised. There they were again, those animals on the run, most of them in human clothing this time, and those humans up against it; here was the slight mistake that led to disaster, here was the fatal accident; this was a world of frozen corpses, dead gophers, snow, dead children, and the ever-present feeling of menace, not from an enemy set over against you but from everything surrounding you. The familiar peril lurked behind every bush, and *I knew the names of the bushes*. Again, I wasn't reading this as Canlit, I was just reading it; I remember being elated by some stories (notably James Reaney's "The Bully") and not very interested in others. But these stories felt real to me in a way that Charles Dickens, much as I enjoyed him, did not.

I've talked about these early experiences not because I think that they were typical but because I think that – significantly – they weren't: I doubt that many people my age had even this much contact, minimal and accidental though it was, with their own literature. (Talking about this now makes me feel about 102, because quite a lot has changed since then. But though new curricula are being invented here and there across the country, I'm not convinced that the *average* Canadian child or high-school student is likely to run across much more Canadian literature than I did. *Why* this is true is of course one of our problems.)

Still, although I didn't read much Canadian writing, what I did read had a shape of its own that felt different from the shapes of the other things I was reading. What that shape turned out to be, and what I felt it meant in terms of this country, became clearer to me the more I read; it is, of course, the subject of this book.

---<o>---

I'd like to begin with a sweeping generalization and argue that every country or culture has a single unifying and informing symbol at its core. (Please don't take any of my oversimplifications as articles of dogma which allow of no exceptions; they are proposed simply to create vantage points from which the literature may be viewed.) The symbol, then – be it word, phrase, idea, image, or all of these – functions like a system of beliefs (it *is* a system of beliefs, though not always a formal one) which holds the country together and helps the people in it to co-operate for common ends. Possibly the symbol for America is The Frontier, a flexible idea that contains many elements dear to the American heart: it suggests a place that is *new*, where the old order can be discarded (as it was when America was instituted by a crop of disaffected Protestants, and later at the time of the Revolution); a line that is always expanding, taking in or "conquering" ever-fresh virgin territory (be it The West, the rest of the world, outer space, Poverty or The Regions of the Mind); it holds out a hope, never fulfilled but always promised, of Utopia, the perfect human society. Most twentieth century American literature is about the gap between the promise and the actuality, between the imagined ideal Golden West or City Upon a Hill, the model for all the world postulated by the Puritans, and the actual squalid materialism, dotty small town, nasty city, or redneck-filled outback. Some Americans have even confused the actuality with the promise: in that case Heaven is a Hilton hotel with a Coke machine in it.

The corresponding symbol for England is perhaps The Island, convenient for obvious reasons. In the seventeenth century a poet called Phineas Fletcher wrote a long poem called *The Purple Island*, which is based on an extended body-as-island metaphor, and, dreadful though the poem is, that's the kind of island I mean: island-as-body, self-contained, a Body Politic, evolving organically, with a hierarchical structure in which the King is the Head, the statesmen the hands, the peasants or farmers or workers the feet, and so on. The Englishman's home as his castle is the popular form of this symbol, the feudal castle being not only an insular structure but a self-contained microcosm of the entire Body Politic.

The central symbol for Canada – and this is based on numerous instances of its occurrence in both English and French Canadian literature – is undoubtedly Survival, *la Survivance*. Like the Frontier and The Island, it is a multi-faceted and adaptable idea. For early explorers and settlers, it meant bare survival in the face of "hostile" elements and/ or natives: carving out a place and a way of keeping alive. But the word can also suggest survival of a crisis or disaster, like a hurricane or a wreck, and many Canadian poems have this kind of survival as a theme; what you might call "grim" survival as opposed to "bare" survival. For French Canada after the English took over it became cultural survival, hanging on as a people, retaining a religion and a language under an alien government. And in English Canada now while the Americans are taking over it is acquiring a similar meaning. There is another use of the word as well: a survival can be a vestige of a vanished order which has managed to persist after its time is past, like a primitive reptile. This version crops up in Canadian thinking too, usually among those who believe that Canada is obsolete.

But the main idea is the first one: hanging on, staying alive. Canadians are forever taking the national pulse like doctors at a sickbed: the aim is not to see whether the patient will live well but simply whether he will live at all. Our central idea is one which generates, not the excitement and sense of adventure or danger which The Frontier holds out, not the smugness and/or sense of security, of everything in its place, which The Island can offer, but an almost intolerable anxiety. Our stories are likely to be tales not of those who made it but of those who made it back from the awful experience – the North, the snowstorm, the sinking ship – that killed everyone else. The survivor has no triumph or victory but the fact of his survival; he has little after his ordeal that he did not have before, except gratitude for having escaped with his life.

A preoccupation with one's survival is necessarily also a preoccupation with the obstacles to that survival. In earlier writers these obstacles are external – the land, the climate, and so forth. In later writers the obstacles tend to become both harder to identify and more internal; they are no longer obstacles to physical survival but obstacles to what we may call spiritual survival, to life as anything more than a minimally human being. Sometimes fear of these obstacles becomes itself the obstacle, and a character is paralyzed by terror (either of what he thinks is threatening him from the outside, or of elements in his own nature that threaten him from within). It may even be life itself that he fears; and when life becomes a threat to life, you have a moderately vicious circle. If a man feels he can survive only by amputating himself, turning himself into a cripple or a eunuch, what price survival?

Just to give you a quick sample of what I'm talking about, here are a few capsule Canadian plots. Some contain attempts to survive which fail. Some contain bare survivals. Some contain crippled successes (the character does more than survive, but is mutilated in the process).

Pratt: *The Titanic*: Ship crashes into iceberg. Most passengers drown.

Pratt: *Brébeuf and His Brethren*: After crushing ordeals, priests survive briefly and are massacred by Indians.

Laurence: *The Stone Angel*: Old woman hangs on grimly to life and dies at the end.

Carrier: *Is It the Sun, Philibert?* Hero escapes incredible rural poverty and horrid urban conditions, almost makes it financially, dies when he wrecks his car.

Marlyn: *Under the Ribs of Death*: Hero amputates himself spiritually in order to make it financially, fails anyway.

Ross: *As For Me and My House*: Prairie minister who hates his job and has crippled himself artistically by sticking with it is offered a dubious chance of escape at the end.

Buckler: *The Mountain and the Valley*: Writer who has been unable to write has vision of possibility at the end but dies before he can implement it.

Gibson: *Communion*: Man who can no longer make human contact tries to save sick dog, fails, and is burned up at the end.

And just to round things out, we might add that the two English Canadian feature films (apart from Allan King's documentaries) to have had much success so far, *Goin' Down the Road* and *The Rowdyman*, are both dramatizations of failure. The heroes survive, but just barely; they are born losers, and their failure to do anything but keep alive has nothing to do with the Maritime Provinces or "regionalism." It's pure Canadian, from sea to sea.

My sample plots are taken from both prose and poetry, and from regions all across Canada; they span four decades, from the thirties to the early seventies. And they hint at another facet of Survivalism: at some point the failure to survive, or the failure to achieve anything beyond survival, becomes not a necessity imposed by a hostile outside world but a choice made from within. Pushed far enough, the obsession with surviving can become the will *not* to survive.

Certainly Canadian authors spend a disproportionate amount of time making sure that their heroes die or fail. Much Canadian writing suggests that failure is required because it is felt – consciously or unconsciously – to be the only "right" ending, the only thing that will support the characters' (or their authors') view of the universe. When such endings are well-handled and consistent with the whole book, one can't quarrel with them on aesthetic grounds. But when Canadian writers are writing clumsy or manipulated endings, they are much less likely to manipulate in a positive than they are in a negative direction: that is, the author is less likely to produce a sudden inheritance from a rich old uncle or the surprising news that his hero is really the son of a Count than he is to conjure up an unexpected natural disaster or an out-of-control car, tree or minor character so that the protagonist may achieve a satisfactory *failure*. Why should this be so? Could it be that Canadians have a will to lose which is as strong and pervasive as the Americans' will to win?

It might be argued that, since most Canlit has been written in the twentieth century and since the twentieth century has produced a generally pessimistic or "ironic" literature, Canada has simply been reflecting a trend. Also, though it's possible to write a short lyric poem about joy and glee, no novel of any length can exclude all but these elements. A novel about unalloyed happiness would have to be either very short or very boring: "Once upon a time John and Mary lived happily ever after, The End." Both of these arguments have some validity, but surely the Canadian gloom is more unrelieved than most and the death and failure toll out of proportion. Given a choice of the negative or positive aspects of any symbol – sea as life-giving Mother, sea as what your ship goes down in; tree as symbol of growth, tree as what falls on your head – Canadians show a marked preference for the negative.

You might decide at this point that most Canadian authors with any pretensions to seriousness are neurotic or morbid, and settle down instead for a good read with *Anne of Green Gables* (though it's about an orphan . . .). But if the coincidence intrigues you – so many writers in such a small country, and *all with the same neurosis* – then I will offer you a theory. Like any theory it won't explain everything, but it may give you some points of departure.

———◇———

Let us suppose, for the sake of argument, that Canada as a whole is a victim, or an "oppressed minority," or "exploited." Let us suppose in short that Canada is a colony. A partial definition of a colony is that it is a place from which a profit is made, but *not by the people who live there*: the major profit from a colony is made in the centre of the empire. That's what colonies are for, to make money for the "mother country," and that's what – since the days of Rome and, more recently, of the Thirteen Colonies – they have always been for. Of course there are cultural side effects which are often identified as "the colonial mentality," and it is these which are examined here; but the root cause for them is economic.

If Canada is a collective victim, it should pay some attention to the Basic Victim Positions. These are like the basic positions in ballet or the scales on the piano: they are primary, though all kinds of song-and-dance variations on them are possible.

The positions are the same whether you are a victimized country, a victimized minority group or a victimized individual.

Basic Victim Positions

Position One: To deny the fact that you are a victim.

This uses up a lot of energy, as you must spend much time explaining away the obvious, suppressing anger, and pretending that certain visible facts do not exist. The position is usually taken by those in a Victim group who are a little better off than the others in that group. They are afraid to recognize they are victims for fear of losing the privileges they possess, and they are forced to account somehow for the disadvantages suffered by the rest of the people in the group by disparaging them. As in: "*I* made it, therefore it's obvious we aren't victims. The rest are just lazy (or neurotic, or stupid); anyway it's their own fault if they aren't happy, look at all the opportunities available for them!"

If anger is felt by Victims in Position One, it is likely to be directed against one's fellow-victims, particularly those who try to talk about their victimization.

The basic game in Position One is "Deny your Victim-experience."

Position Two:

> *To acknowledge the fact that you are a victim, but to explain*
> *this as an act of Fate, the Will of God, the dictates of Biology*
> *(in the case of women, for instance), the necessity decreed*
> *by History, or Economics, or the Unconscious, or any other*
> *large general powerful idea.*

In any case, since it is the fault of this large *thing* and not your
own fault, you can neither be blamed for your position nor
be expected to do anything about it. You can be resigned and
long-suffering, or you can kick against the pricks and make a
fuss; in the latter case your rebellion will be deemed foolish or
evil even by you, and you will expect to lose and be punished,
for who can fight Fate (or the Will of God, or Biology)?

Notice that:

1. The explanation *displaces* the cause from the real source
of oppression to something else.

2. Because the fake cause is so vast, nebulous and unchangeable, you are permanently excused from changing it, *and also*
from deciding how much of your situation (e.g. the climate) is
unchangeable, how much can be changed, and how much is
caused by habit or tradition or your own need to be a victim.

3. Anger, when present – or scorn, since everyone in the
category is defined as inferior – is directed against both
fellow-victims and oneself.

The basic game in Position Two is Victor/Victim.

Position Three:

To acknowledge the fact that you are a victim but to refuse to accept the assumption that the role is inevitable.

As in: "Look what's being done to me, and it isn't Fate, it isn't the Will of God. Therefore I can stop seeing myself as a *fated* Victim."

To put it differently: you can distinguish between the *role* of Victim (which probably leads you to seek victimization even when there's no call for it), and the *objective experience* that is making you a victim. And you can probably go further and decide how much of the objective experience could be changed if you made the effort.

This is a dynamic position, rather than a static one; from it you can move on to Position Four, but if you become locked into your anger and fail to change your situation, you might well find yourself back in Position Two.

Notice that:

1. In this position the real cause of oppression is for the first time identified.

2. Anger can be directed against the real source of oppression, and energy channelled into constructive action.

3. You can make real decisions about how much of your position can be changed and how much can't (you can't make it stop snowing; you can stop blaming the snow for everything that's wrong).

The basic game of Position Three is repudiating the Victim role.

Position Four: To be a creative non-victim.

Strictly speaking, Position Four is a position not for victims but for those who have never been victims at all, or for ex-victims: those who have been able to move into it from Position Three because the external and/or the internal causes of victimization have been removed. (In an oppressed society, of course, you can't become an ex-victim – insofar as you are connected with your society – until the entire society's position has been changed.)

In Position Four, creative activity of all kinds becomes possible. Energy is no longer being suppressed (as in Position One) or used up for displacement of the cause, or for passing your victimization along to others (Man kicks Child, Child kicks Dog) as in Position Two; nor is it being used for the dynamic anger of Position Three. And you are able to accept your own experience for what it is, rather than having to distort it to make it correspond with others' versions of it (particularly those of your oppressors).

In Position Four, Victor/Victim games are obsolete. You don't even have to concentrate on rejecting the role of Victim, because the role is no longer a temptation for you.

(There may be a Position Five, for mystics; I postulate it but will not explore it here, since mystics do not as a rule write books.)

I devised this model not as the Secret of Life or the answer to everything (though you can apply it to world politics or your friends if you like), but as a helpful method of approaching our literature. It's a model about Victims for the simple reason that I found a superabundance of victims in Canadian literature. If I'd been looking at the nineteenth century English novel I'd have devised a table called Characteristics of Gentlemen; or if I'd been investigating American literature I would have found myself thinking about picaresque anti-heroes; or if I'd been examining German Romantic literature the result would probably have been a diagram of Doppelgängers. But stick a pin in Canadian literature at random, and nine times out of ten you'll hit a victim. My model, then, is a product of my Canadian literary experiences, not a Procrustean bed dreamed up in advance on which Canlit is about to be stretched. Now that I've traced its main outlines, I'll indicate briefly how I intend to use – and not to use – the model.

First, three general points about the model:

- As I said, this is a verbal diagram: it is intended to be suggestive rather than totally accurate. But experience is never this linear: you're rarely in any Position in its pure form for very long – and you may have a foot, as it were, in more than one Position at once.
- What happens to an individual who has reached Position Three in a society which is still in Positions One or Two? (Not very nice things, usually.) Or, what happens to an individual who is a victim – like a Black in America – in a society which as a whole is *not* being oppressed by another society? (Again, not very nice things.) If, for instance, your society is in Position Two, perhaps you can't move through Position Three into Position Four except

by repudiating your society, or at least its assumptions about the nature of life and proper behaviour. This may eventually make Position Four unreal for you: can you fiddle happily while Rome groans?

- I've presented the model as though it were based on individual rather than social experience. Perhaps the terms would shift slightly if you were to substitute "we" or "our class" or "our country" for "I," and you'd then get a more complicated analysis of Canadian colonialism. My approach is more modest: it sketches a perspective from which Canadian *Literature* makes a surprising amount of sense.

Now, the model as it applies to writing:

- I assume that *by definition* (mine, and you don't have to believe me) an author is in Position Four at the moment of writing, that is, the moment of creation – though the subject of his book may be Position Two, and the energy for it may come from Position Three. In the rest of his life he shifts around, like everyone else. (The analogous Position Four moment for the reader is not the time it takes to read a book, but the moment of insight – the time when the book makes sense or comes clear.) And apart from that comment, I don't want to speculate about the state of authors' souls. Instead, just as in the Preface I proposed the fiction that the literature was being written by Canada, I here propose to regard novels and poems as though they were expressions of Positions, not of authors.
- This method will, I hope, articulate the skeleton of Canadian literature. It will let you see how the bones fit together, but it won't put flesh on them. That is, the

method provides a static dissection, rather than a dynamic examination of a process-in-motion. (A "static" model facilitates classification. Trying out a dynamic model would also be interesting.)

- Because I'm not handing out gold stars, I'll try not to do much evaluating – praising or censuring – of books according to this model. Although in real life Position Four may be preferable to Position Two, I do find a consistent and tough-minded Position Two poem preferable to a sloppy and unearned Position Four one. But I'll let you do that kind of evaluation for yourself.

You might try to decide whether, in any given work, the actual conditions of the characters' lives are sufficient to account for the doom and gloom meted out to them. Bare Survival isn't a central theme by accident, and neither is the victim motif; the land *was* hard, and we have been (and are) an exploited colony; our literature is rooted in those facts. But you might wonder, in a snowstorm-kills-man story, whether the snowstorm is an adequate explanation for the misery of the characters, or whether the author has displaced the source of the misery in their world and is blaming the snowstorm when he ought to be blaming something else. If so, it is a Position Two story: quite apart from the subject matter, it expresses a premature resignation and a misplaced willingness to see one's victimization as unchangeable.

And I'll point out too that a book can be a symptom or reflection of a Position (though not necessarily a bad book); or it can be a *conscious examination* of it (though not necessarily a good one). The latter seems less fatalistic; a conscious examination of victim experience – including the *need* to be a victim – suggests a more realistic desire to transcend the experience, even if that is not made explicit in the book.

———◄○►———

I've laid out the skeleton of Canadian literature in a way that was easy for me to manage and I hope will be easy for you to follow. The key patterns themselves are arranged in four groups. Chapters Two, Three and Four (the first group) deal with the patterns Canadian literature has made of what white people found when they arrived here: the land, the animals, and the Indians. Chapters Five, Six, Seven and Eight deal with what Canadian literature has made of its "ancestor" figures. Chapters Nine and Ten cope with two representative figures – the Canadian Artist, who is usually male, and the Canadian Woman, who is usually female – and explore some of the reasons for their rather curtailed anatomies. And Chapters Eleven and Twelve provide some rays of light, in the shape of bonfires and insights.

You will need the rays of light because the surrounding gloom sometimes gets pretty dense; a lot of our literature (as you may have suspected) is either an expression or an examination of Position Two: "I am a victim but there is nothing I can do about it." However, a writer's job is to tell his society not how it ought to live, but how it does live.

But before you plunge in here are some cheering thoughts:

- Although negative stances towards theme and image predominate, there are also examples of escapes, positive changes, and revelations.
- Much of our literature is a diagram of what is *not* desired. Knowing what you don't want isn't the same as knowing what you do want, but it helps.

- Naming your own condition, your own disease, is not necessarily the same as acquiescing in it. Diagnosis is the first step.

Armed with these maxims, you should be proof against some of the murkier depths that lie ahead.

APPENDIX: HISTORY AND NATIONALISM

For two quick views of Canadian history, both in the form of comic books, see:

She Named It Canada. The Corrective Collective, 421 East 48th Ave., Vancouver, B.C. $0.50. (Bulk orders of 50 or more, $0.35.)

The History of Quebec. Léandre Bergeron and Robert Lavaill; English or French; NC Press, P.O. Box 6106, Terminal A, Toronto 116. $1.00.

There's also *The Boreal Express*, Canadian history in newspaper format, available from Clarke Irwin, 10 issues for $5.00.

Four books which are helpful in connection with the theoretical parts of this chapter are:

George Grant, *Technology and Empire*; AN, $2.50.

Ian Lumsden, ed., *Close the 49th Parallel: The Americanization of Canada*; UTP, $3.75.

Kari Levitt, *Silent Surrender*; Macmillan, $3.50.

Glen Frankfurter, *Baneful Domination*; Longman ($11.50; not in paper yet).

For a more extensive list, see the one following the chapter "Foreign Control of the Economy" in *Read Canadian* (ed. Godfrey, Fulford and Rotstein); James Lewis and Samuel, $1.95.

2

NATURE THE MONSTER

I have long been impressed in Canadian poetry by a tone of deep terror in regard to nature. . . . It is not a terror of the dangers or discomforts or even the mysteries of nature, but a terror of the soul at something that these things manifest.

– *Northrop Frye,*
The Bush Garden

Whether alive or dead the bush resisted:
Alive, it must be slain with axe and saw,
If dead, it was in tangle at their feet.
The ice could hit men as it hit the spruces.
Even the rivers had betraying tricks. . . .

– *E. J. Pratt,*
Towards the Last Spike

. . . Nature is just a lot of waste and cruelty, maybe not from Nature's point of view but from a human point of view. Cruelty is the law of Nature.

– *Alice Munro,*
Lives of Girls and Women

. . . But now
That the forests are cut down, the rivers charted,
Where can you turn, where can you travel? Unless
Through the desperate wilderness behind your eyes,
So full of falls and glooms and desolations . . .

– *Douglas LePan,*
"Coureurs de bois"

... the world is a leafless wood; we stare
abruptly upon tundra and the sky –
soul's frontiers where we meet,
knowing ourselves only
capacities for loneliness,
solitudes wherein the barrens sound.

– D. G. Jones,
"Soliloquy to Absent Friends"

———

When one contemplates the conquest of nature by technology one must remember that that conquest had to include our own bodies. Calvinism provided the determined and organized men and women who could rule the mastered world. The punishment they inflicted on non-human nature, they had first inflicted on themselves.

– George Grant,
Technology and Empire

Poems which contain descriptions of landscapes and natural objects are often dismissed as being mere Nature poetry. But Nature poetry is seldom just about Nature; it is usually about the poet's *attitude* towards the external natural universe. That is, landscapes in poems are often interior landscapes; they are maps of a state of mind. Sometimes the poem conceals this fact and purports to be objective description, sometimes the poem acknowledges and explores the interior landscape it presents. The same tendencies can be present in the descriptive passages of novels or stories with natural settings. What we are looking at in this chapter is the types of landscape that prevail in Canadian literature and the kinds of attitude they mirror.

Not surprisingly in a country with such a high ratio of trees, lakes and rocks to people, images from Nature are almost everywhere. Added up, they depict a Nature that is often dead and unanswering or actively hostile to man; or, seen in its gentler spring and summer aspects, unreal. There is a sense in Canadian literature that the true and only season here is winter: the others are either preludes to it or mirages concealing it. There is a three-line poem by Alden Nowlan called "April in New Brunswick" which puts this case perfectly:

> Spring is distrusted here, for it deceives –
> snow melts upon the lawns, uncovering
> last fall's dead leaves.

The key word is "distrusted"; Canadian writers as a whole do not trust Nature, they are always suspecting some dirty trick. An often-encountered sentiment is that Nature has betrayed expectation, it was supposed to be different.

This distrust, this sense of betrayal, may be traced in part to expectations which were literary in origin. English Canada

45

was settled first, but sparsely, in the eighteenth century; a larger influx of immigrants from England arrived during the first half of the nineteenth century. The prevailing literary mode in Nature poetry in the late eighteenth century as derived from Edmund Burke was the cult of the sublime and the picturesque, featuring views and inspirational scenery. In the first half of the nineteenth century this shifted to Wordsworthian Romanticism. What you were "supposed" to feel about Nature under the first mode was awe at the grandeur of Nature; under the second, you were supposed to feel that Nature was a kind Mother or Nurse who would guide man if he would only listen to her. In the popular mind, the two modes often combined; in any case, Nature was "good" and cities were "evil." Nature the kind Mother on Earth had joined and in some cases replaced God the severe Father in Heaven who had been around for some time previously. In the United States, Emerson and his disciples Thoreau and Whitman are certainly later tributaries of this stream.

Towards the middle of the century Nature's personality underwent a change; she remained a female deity, but she became redder in tooth and claw as Darwinism infiltrated literature. However, most of the English immigrants were by that time safely in Canada, their heads filled with diluted Burke and Wordsworth, encountering lots and lots of Nature. If Wordsworth was right, Canada ought to have been the Great Good Place. At first, complaining about the bogs and mosquitoes must have been like criticizing the authority of the Bible.

Susanna Moodie's description of the "surpassing grandeur" of the view near Grosse Isle reads like a dictionary of early nineteenth-century Nature adjectives:

The previous day had been dark and stormy, and a heavy fog had concealed the mountain chain, which forms the stupendous background to this sublime view, entirely from our sight. As the clouds rolled away from their grey bald brows, and cast into denser shadows the vast forest belts that girdled them round, they loomed out like mighty giants – Titans of the earth, in all their rugged and awful beauty – a thrill of wonder and delight pervaded my mind. The spectacle floated dimly on my sight – my eyes were blinded with tears – blinded by the excess of beauty. I turned to the right and to the left, I looked up and down the glorious river; never had I beheld so many striking objects blended into one mighty whole! Nature had lavished all her noblest features in producing that enchanting scene.

But the tension between what you were officially supposed to feel and what you actually encountered when you got here – and the resultant sense of being gypped – is much in evidence.

In *Roughing It in the Bush*, Mrs. Moodie's determination to preserve her Wordsworthian faith collides with the difficulty she has in doing so when Nature fails time and time again to come through for her. The result is a markedly double-minded attitude towards Canada:

> . . . The aspect of Nature ever did, and I hope ever will, continue: *"To shoot marvellous strength into my heart."* As long as we remain true to the Divine Mother, so long will she remain faithful to her suffering children.
>
> At that period my love for Canada was a feeling very nearly allied to that which the condemned criminal entertains for his cell – his only hope of escape being through the portals of the grave.

Those two emotions – faith in the Divine Mother and a feeling of hopeless imprisonment – follow each other on the page without break or explanation. If the Divine Mother is all that faithful, we may ask, why are her children suffering? Moodie copes with the contradiction by dividing Nature itself in two, reserving the splendid adjectives and the Divine-Mother attributes for the half that she approves of and failing to account for the hostile activities of the other half.

Again and again we find her gazing at the sublime natural goings-on in the misty distance – sunsets, mountains, spectacular views – only to be brought up short by disagreeable things in her immediate foreground, such as bugs, swamps, tree roots and other immigrants. Nature the Sublime can be approached but never reached, and Nature the Divine Mother hardly functions at all; like God she may be believed in but not experienced directly, and she's not much help with the vegetable garden. Unfortunately it's the swamps, bugs, tree roots and other immigrants that form the texture of daily life.

This tension between expectation and actuality was not confined to Mrs. Moodie. It's there as a sense of something missing in the almost surreal interlude in Alexander McLachlan's *The Emigrant*, where a labyrinthine journey through a forest, "Through morasses, over bogs, / Wading rivers, crossing logs," ends in a forest glade filled with unknown and nameless coloured birds, none of which has any "song." (The birds lack songs not because they are mute but because the sounds they make are not like the sounds the emigrant McLachlan is *accustomed* to hearing birds make. It's like a North American listening to Oriental music and hearing only cacophony.) The tension creeps also into Charles Sangster's attempt to cram Canadian scenery into a Nature poem of the saccharine or Leigh Hunt variety. "The St. Lawrence and the Saguenay" oozes along for the most part like this:

Here Nature, lavish of her wealth, did strew
Her flocks of panting islets on the breast
Of the admiring River, where they grew
Like shapes of Beauty, formed to give a zest
To the charmed mind, like waking Visions of the Blest.

But then comes this curious stanza:

Here Nature holds her Carnival of Isles.
Steeped in warm sunlight all the merry day,
Each nodding tree and floating greenwood smiles,
And moss-crowned monsters move in grim array.
All night the Fisher spears his finny prey;
The piney flambeaux reddening the deep,
Past the dim shores, or up some mimic bay:
Like grotesque banditti they boldly sweep
Upon the startled prey, and stab them while they sleep.

Some carnival. The lavishness, panting, merriment and Beauty
hardly account for the "moss-crowned monsters," nor for that
really unexpected stab in the dark. In any other country this
kind of unexplained inconsistency of image might be just bad
poetry; here it's bad poetry *plus*, and the plus is the doubtless
unintended revelation of a split attitude.

   That this kind of tension or split is not just a characteristic
of the nineteenth century is demonstrated in Douglas LePan's
important poem, "A Country Without A Mythology," where
the pattern is almost intact. In it, someone called "the stranger"
is travelling towards no discernible goal through a land without
"monuments or landmarks," among "a savage people" who
are silent and moody or, when they speak, incomprehensi-
ble. "The stranger" must live off the land on berries and fish,
snatching what he can get and "forgetting every grace and

ceremony." What is missing for him in this alien land are the emblems of tradition-saturated European civilization:

> The abbey clock, the dial in the garden,
> Fade like saints' days and festivals.
> Months, years, are here unbroken virgin forests.
> There is no law. . . .

The landscape itself is harsh, "violent," sharp and jagged, bitter cold in winter and burning hot in summer. But the traveller retains his desire for a Wordsworthian experience of Nature as divine and kindly:

> Sometimes – perhaps at the tentative fall of twilight –
> A belief will settle that waiting around the bend
> Are sanctities of childhood, that melting birds
> Will sing him into a limpid gracious Presence.

> The hills will fall in folds, the wilderness
> Will be a garment innocent and lustrous
> To wear upon a birthday, under a light
> That curls and smiles, a golden-haired Archangel.

But somehow this never happens; he continues his journey, but the landscape does not grant him the vision he requires:

> And now the channel opens. But nothing alters.
> Mile after mile of tangled struggling roots,
> Wild-rice, stumps, weeds, that clutch at the canoe,
> Wild birds hysterical in tangled trees.

> And not a sign, no emblem in the sky
> Or boughs to friend him as he goes; for who

Will stop where, clumsily constructed, daubed
With war-paint, teeters some lust-red manitou?

There is, of course, more than one possible interpretation for the ending of this poem. We can believe with "the stranger" that Nature has withheld all revelation, or indeed that Nature is empty, has no revelation to give, no "sign" or "emblem." Or we can take the hint that the poet gives us: perhaps the stranger has been given a revelation but has not been able to recognize it. There *is* an image of the divine present in the landscape – the "manitou" which the Indians have carved – but since the traveller is looking where he has been taught to look, up towards the sky, and since he is demanding that any revelation shall arrive in his terms – terms he has learned in Europe – he misses the real revelation which is there on the ground, and which takes a shape appropriate to the landscape itself, not to his ideas of what it ought to be. Because the mythic figure, "the manitou," is not a "golden-haired Archangel" it is dismissed as clumsy and perhaps even rejected as impure or dangerous – it is, after all, "lust-red." The real point of the manitou may be that, whatever it is, it is *here*, it is actual and possible, whereas the traveller's Wordsworthian and European Christian fantasies are only wishful thinking, and of a destructive kind: they prevent him from making meaningful contact with his actual environment. Perhaps this is why he remains a stranger: he's looking for the wrong thing in the wrong place.

If the Divine Mother is conspicuous by her absence and the vision of a "gracious Presence" steadfastly refuses to manifest itself, the person who demands Divine Mothers and Presences may conclude that Nature is dead (as the late nineteenth century in Europe concluded that God was dead, since He was no longer producing miracles and chariots of fire). Nature seen as dead, or alive but indifferent, or alive and actively hostile towards man is a common image in Canadian literature. The result of a dead or indifferent Nature is an isolated or "alienated" man; the result of an actively hostile Nature is usually a dead man, and certainly a threatened one.

Death by Nature – not to be confused with "natural deaths" such as heart attacks – is an event of startling frequency in Canadian literature; in fact it seems to polish off far more people in literature than it does in real life. In Death by Nature, something in the natural environment murders the individual, though the author – who is of course the real guilty party, since it is he who has arranged the murder – often disguises the foul deed to make it look like an accident.

The Canadian author's two favourite "natural" methods for dispatching his victims are drowning and freezing, drowning being preferred by poets – probably because it can be used as a metaphor for a descent into the unconscious – and freezing by prose writers. Why this should be so is evident if you think about the other methods made available by the actual environment. There is lots of water and snow in Canada, and both are good murder weapons; but other plausible weapons are few. There are no deserts and no jungles. You could kill a man by having a rock fall on him, or having him fall off one (and that's been done, by Earle Birney in *David*). You can squash him under a tree, as Isabella Crawford does in *Malcolm's Katie*, but that's not too effective: the victim recovers. Trees piled in log-jams work better as squashing devices, as in Duncan Campbell Scott's poem "At the Cedars." There aren't many venomous reptiles or vermin in Canada, though rattlesnakes are on the increase; I once read a mystery story in which one of the victims was murdered by being tied to a tree in the blackfly season, but I don't believe it was Canadian. For reasons which have to do with the profundities of the Canadian psyche, Death by Wild

Animal is infrequent. (See Chapter Three.) Death by Indian has something to do with Death by Nature, but it is not quite the same thing. (See Chapter Four.) It would be possible to have someone burn up in a forest fire, but I can't think of any author who's tried this. Death by Nature can also come in the form of suicide, and again drowning and freezing are favourite methods; for the latter, see Sinclair Ross's story "The Painted Door" and (more or less) Duncan Campbell Scott's poem "The Forsaken."

Water and snow, then, are the usual implements, though there's another, more indirect way of doing in a character: Death by Bushing, in which a character isolated in Nature goes crazy. Legends of the Wendigo get connected with this one – the character sees too much of the wilderness, and in a sense becomes it, leaving his humanity behind. Joyce Marshall's story "The Old Woman" contains a madness of this kind. Another good example is Earle Birney's poem "Bushed," in which the protagonist at first lives well enough within Nature, but then comes to feel that the mountain beside which he has built his shack is alive and unfriendly towards him:

> But the moon carved unknown totems
> out of the lakeshore
> owls in the beardusky woods derided him
> moosehorned cedars circled his swamps and tossed
> their antlers up to the stars
> Then he knew though the mountain slept the winds
> were shaping its peak to an arrowhead
> poised
>
> And now he could only
> bar himself in and wait
> for the great flint to come singing into his heart

The attitudes towards Death by Nature vary, as do the amounts of guilt or responsibility ascribed to Nature. At one end of the spectrum is the fatalism displayed in F. P. Grove's story "Snow." The story is simple to the point of aridity: a man living at the edge of civilization is missing in the snow and some other men set out to find him. They discover his dead body frozen stiff. They announce the news to his wife, who is left destitute with six children, and to his parents. His mother-in-law, collapsing into tears, says "God's will be done." The death is presented as a fact, as the kind of thing that happens; no attempt is made to explain it or soften it and the woman's exclamation is, in context, ironic. Here Nature is dead or indifferent rather than actively hostile: it is a condition, not a person.

Death by Nature has a somewhat different aspect in Earle Birney's long poem *David*. On the surface the poem is about two young men who go mountain-climbing. They want to try a peak, called "the Finger," which they've never climbed before. When they reach the top the narrator slips and his friend David reaches to steady him, but falls to a ledge. The narrator climbs down to him, finds him crushed but still alive, and at David's insistence pushes him over the ledge to smash on the ice six hundred feet below. The death of David is ostensibly a kind of accident, and any guilt for it belongs to the narrator, who caused David's fall by his carelessness (he didn't test his footholds) and, more directly, by pushing him over.

But the imagery of the poem casts a different light on the story. The Finger itself is an anthropomorphic form: it is at first "an overhang / Crooked like a talon." This could be the talon of a bird, but later it is overtly humanoid: after the accident the narrator says, "Above us climbed the last joint of the Finger / Beckoning bleakly the wide indifferent sky." The sky may be indifferent, but the Finger isn't: it beckons, and in a sense it is

the beckoning of the Finger that has lured David to his de
isn't the only giant hand present: in the second section, another
peak is "like a fist in a frozen ocean of rock. . . ." The Divine
Mother's hands are scarcely extended in blessing.

An interesting thing about the images in *David* is the way
they change from Nature-is-indifferent images before David's
fall to Nature-is-hostile images after it. Before the fall, there is
a whole group of images that connect mountains with ocean:
there's the "frozen ocean of rock" just mentioned, "a long
green surf of junipers," the "ice in the morning thaw" that is
"a gurgling world of crystal and cold blue chasms, / And seracs
that shone like frozen saltgreen waves." More explicitly, there
is David's knowledge of geology, which reveals that the mountains *were* an ocean once: the fossils of coral and trilobites
are "Letters delivered to man from the Cambrian waves." Ice,
ocean and rock are pulled together by these images; the total
picture is of a Nature which is huge and "unknowing" but not
actively trying to destroy. It is the narrator's innocence which
makes such a vision possible; had he been more suspicious of
the Divine Mother he would have paid more attention to the
mangled bodies of her children which the two climbers encounter: the skeleton of a mountain goat that has slipped, and a
maimed robin.

After David's fall, which is also a fall from grace – from a
vision of Nature as at least indifferent and sometimes beautiful,
a Nature that man may exist in and enjoy if he is strong and
careful – the images change. David is found with "a cruel fang"
of stone poking into him; his blood is being drunk by "thirsting
lichens." The landscape the narrator has passed through earlier
on the way to the Finger is crossed by him again on his way
back, but this time the chimney he must descend is "an empty
horror," the snow is "sun-cankered," the crevasses are "gaping"

and "greenthroated," the seracs are "fanged," the glacier has a "snout." Even on more solid ground the swamp that had earlier "quivered with frogsong" is now "ragged"; it reeks, and its toadstools are "obscene." The landscape has come alive; it is no longer an ocean but a body, the body of a vampire or cannibal or ghoul, with its fangs and bloodthirsty lichens and its stench of decay. David's fall into death is the narrator's fall into a vision of Nature as a destructive and hideous monster.

David's name is suggestive: where there is a David in Canadian literature there is usually a Goliath, and the Goliath, the evil giant (or giantess) is, of course, Nature herself. David has been challenging it to combat by fighting his way up the mountains, but as in many Canadian David-and-Goliath stories, Goliath wins.

Goliath wins again, and even more tellingly, in E. J. Pratt's long poem *The Titanic*: and with these winning-and-losing metaphors it's obvious that we have left behind the fatalistic attitude that goes with "Nature is dead or indifferent" and are dealing with a war-with-Nature or let's-fight attitude that goes with "Nature is hostile."

The Titanic itself – as its name implies – is a giant created by man as a challenge to Nature; this is made obvious by Pratt in the second section of the poem, in which the ship is spoken of as having "lungs" and a "heart," and in which the belief in her indestructibility is seen as yet another example of man's attempt to defy the universe:

> And this belief had reached its climax when,
> Through wireless waves as yet unstaled by use,
> The wonder of the ether had begun
> To fold the heavens up and reinduce
> That ancient *hubris* in the hearts of men,

Which would have slain the cattle of the sun,
And filched the lightnings from the fist of Zeus.

The Titanic is also a kind of Noah's Ark, carrying a microcosm
of the society that has created it, from the rich on the upper
decks to the immigrants in the steerage. It is human civilization in miniature, setting out to conquer Goliath; but instead
of saving its passengers from the Flood it drowns them in it.

The description of the iceberg that sinks the Titanic is worth
some attention. It is not alive (though at the moment of col-
lision there is "No shock! No more than if something alive /
had brushed her. . . ."), it is a "thing" with the blind, uncaring
motions and attributes of a thing; and as "thing" it embodies
the three elements of the physical universe we found also in
David: ice or snow, ocean and rock. (Here the ice of the berg
is seen as rock, whereas in *David* mountain rock was seen as
ocean.) Yet it is given two metaphorical identities. The first,
with its images of European church architecture, suggests the
wish for the "gracious Presence" version of Nature longed for
in LePan's poem:

> Pressure and glacial time had stratified
> The berg to the consistency of flint,
> And kept inviolate, through clash of tide
> And gale, facade and columns with their hint
> Of inward altars and of steepled bells. . . .

But this identity is only external; the berg erodes until "the last
temple touch of grace" is gone, and under its facade are no
"inward altars" but only "the brute / And paleolithic outline
of a face." The face is that of a monster, half shambling beast,
half human; the monster has a claw, and it is this claw that rips

57

open the Titanic. Nature's Goliath proves much bigger and stronger than the puny David which has been sent against it; at the end of the poem, when the moments of human courage or panic have come and gone on the sinking ship, the ice titan remains, virtually unmoved:

> And out there in the starlight, with no trace
> Upon it of its deed but the last wave
> From the Titanic fretting at its base,
> Silent, composed, ringed by its icy broods,
> The grey shape with the paleolithic face
> Was still the master of the longitudes.

This monster is of uncertain sex ("broods" and "master" seem to contradict each other) but the Nature-monster in another Pratt poem, *Towards the Last Spike*, is definitely female. Female Nature-monsters are examined at length in Chapter Ten; suffice it to say that the monster in *Towards the Last Spike* is the Canadian Shield in the form of a female dragon or lizard, that war is declared against her by Sir John A. Macdonald and takes the form of building a railroad through her, that she fights back with the weapons at her disposal, namely the traditional ones of ice, rock and water (also trees, dead and alive), and that this time tiny man wins the war against the giant.

A curious thing starts happening in Canadian literature once man starts winning, once evidence starts piling up of what Frye in *The Bush Garden* calls "the conquest of nature by an intelligence that does not love it." Sympathy begins to shift from the victorious hero to the defeated giantess, and the problem is no longer how to avoid being swallowed up by a cannibalistic Nature but how to avoid destroying her.

The war against Nature assumed that Nature was hostile to

begin with; man could fight and lose, or he could fight and win. If he won he would be rewarded: he could conquer and enslave Nature, and, in practical terms, exploit her resources. But it is increasingly obvious to some writers that man is now more destructive towards Nature than Nature can be towards man; and, furthermore, that the destruction of Nature is equivalent to self-destruction on the part of man. Earle Birney has a poem dating from 1945 called "Transcontinental," which is a sort of *Towards the Last Spike* revisited. In it the narrator is going across Canada in a plushy train, "crawling across this some-time garden," surrounded by colourful tourist folders; when he looks out the window he sees "this great green girl grown sick / with man sick with the likes of us. . . ." The land is a woman again, but this time a "girl," not a monster; human beings are parasites on her body, and she is covered with scars, scum and other evidences of disease. Birney's conclusion is not that the Divine Mother will forgive, but that man will have to clean up the mess he has made:

> It is true she is too big and strong to die
> of this disease but she grows quickly old
> this lady   old with us –
> nor have we any antibodies for her aid
> except her own.

You may not like the disease-and-cure terminology, but at least it's revealing; the power is no longer with Nature, Birney indicates, it's with man.

Man-the-aggressor is taken a step further in Peter Such's novel *Fallout*, in which the rape of the land by an impious machine technology finally provokes retaliation by Nature, in the form of a hurricane. Nature's hostility here is not unprovoked; it is seen as retribution, punishment for a crime. The moral weight – and the author's identification – is definitely on the side of Nature.

Dennis Lee goes even further in *Civil Elegies*. He implies that the result of the North American war on Nature is not an enhancing of human civilization but a stunting of it – and that the ripoff policies towards the land, which have gone hand-in-hand with the Nature-is-hostile stance, issue eventually in the death of cities as well.

> For a people which lays its whiskey and violent
> > machines
> on a land that is primal, and native, which takes
> > that land in greedy
> innocence but will not live it, which is not claimed by
> > its own
> and sells that land off even before it has owned it. . . .
>
> that people will botch its cities, its greatest squares
> will scoff at its money and stature, and prising wide
> a civil space to live in, by the grace of its own
> > invention it will
> fill that space with the artifacts of death.

Without pushing it, I'd like to look at some ways in which the attitudes towards Nature we've been noticing might fit into what I said earlier about the Basic Victim Positions. And I'll say, incidentally and to avoid misunderstanding, that a poem – unlike a politician – must be judged not on what position it takes but on how well it "does" that position.

Pretending that Nature is the all-good Divine Mother when you're being eaten by mosquitoes and falling into bogs is Position One. It can't really stand up very long against the

Canadian climate and the Canadian terrain, measured against which Wordsworth's Lake District – Divine Mother country – is merely a smallish lukewarm pimple. So most of our Position One Nature poetry is nineteenth century.

There are several variations of Position Two. As I said before, acknowledging the truth of your situation is always preferable to concealing it; so poems that talk about the hardness of the land and the difficulties of coming to terms with it are a desirable first step. Merely to describe *where* it is you are and *what* that looks and feels like is a relief if you've been conned into believing something different; it's like the small boy and the Emperor's New Clothes. If it's cold, say so – name your condition out loud. In a lot of early Canadian poetry you find this desire to *name* struggling against a terminology which is foreign and completely inadequate to describe what is actually being seen. Part of the delight of reading Canadian poetry chronologically is watching the gradual emergence of a language appropriate to its objects. I'd say it first began to really happen in poets such as Lampman and Duncan Campbell Scott. For a good example, take a look at A. J. M. Smith's poem "The Lonely Land," which has all the jagged edges of a Tom Thompson jack pine but still manages to affirm.

Position Two writing is not always able to reach ahead to Positions Three and Four. Naming a Nature which is not like the one you expected can lead to the feeling that Nature is dead or indifferent, and from there to the feeling that Nature is alive and actively hostile towards man. And such attitudes *can* be symptomatic of some other unstated attitudes that have to do with living in a colony. That is, "Nature is dead" can mean "Things don't look the way they are supposed to, that is, the way they did 'at home.' Therefore I am in exile." And "Nature is hostile and is out to get me" *can* mean also "I feel small, helpless and victimized. I seem to have little power over my own destiny.

Something must be doing this to me but I can't put my finger on a concrete enemy. Therefore the enemy must be Nature."

You can easily see how the Position Two feeling that Nature is a huge powerful hostile enemy against whom man will lose can turn into the *will to lose*. Instead of "Chances are Nature will win because it's bigger" you get "I will lose – I *must* lose – because that's the way things are and ought to be." Man wills his role as victim because this completes for him a Universe-as-hostile pattern, and at this point the pattern becomes self-perpetuating. Wherever it comes from, this attitude sees mainly the obstacles to our survival, and it can itself become an obstacle to survival.

Deciding to "win the war against Nature" can move you into Position Three ("Being a victim is not foreordained; I refuse to be a victim"). But as in all apparent moves into Position Three, the Position Two pattern may continue with merely a change of roles. Instead of giant Nature beating up weak helpless man, we get giant man beating up weak helpless Nature, and there's just as much chance to play victim if you then identify with Nature and see the plight as inescapable. ("Pollution will get us all in twenty years. There's nothing we can do but SUFFER.") That lands you right back in Position Two, helpless and doomed. Again, naming the awful truth is necessary, but postulating it as inevitable leads to impotence and futility. The real Position Three move that will get you to Position Four is probably "I refuse to play Victor/Victim with Nature" – a rejection of war games.

What is natural is not always external. As George Grant points out in the quotation at the beginning of this chapter, attitudes towards Nature inevitably involve man's attitude towards his own body and towards sexuality, insofar as these too are seen as part of Nature. It doesn't take much thought to deduce what "Nature is dead" and "Nature is hostile" are going to do to a man's attitudes towards his own body and towards women; you'll find some related evidence in Chapters Nine and Ten.

What does Nature look like from Position Four? Well, it isn't the Divine Mother – that is, it isn't all-good – and it isn't Nature the evil monster. It exists as itself, I suspect, but not as a collection of separate and inert objects; rather it exists as a living process which includes opposites: life and death, "gentleness" and "hostility."

From Position Four, man himself is seen as part of the process; he does not define himself as "good" or "weak" as against a hostile Nature, or as "bad" or "aggressive" as against a passive, powerless Nature. He can accept his own body, including its sexuality, as part of this process, accepting too the versatility that the process requires. Since he does not see life as something that can only be maintained inside a fortress and at the expense of shutting out Nature and sex, he is free to move *within* space rather than in a self-created tank *against* it.

Such moments are few in Canadian poetry, but they do exist, they are imaginable and therefore possible. They occur significantly, for instance, in the work of Irving Layton. In his "social" poems Layton is usually locked into Position Three anger, trying rather frantically to dissociate himself from the grey sterile Position Two Canadian WASPS and fat rich Position One Jews he sets up as straw men. A lot of those poems are "I'm-not-like-them" poems, and his strident insistence that we take note of his balls as though of some rare novelty would be tedious if it weren't such a helpful key to a real national anxiety. Much of the time he accepts the Victor/Victim game, but makes the un-Canadian choice of identifying with the victors rather than the victims. However, in some of the Nature poems he transcends those alternatives and moves into the processes of life-as-energy. In "For Mao Tse-Tung: A Meditation on Flies and Kings," he squashes flies and "derides" bushes while also being able to experience "ecstasy" in his identification with sun and forest. And in "The Birth of Tragedy" he says,

> In me, nature's divided things –
>   tree, mould on tree –
>   have their fruition;
> I am their core. Let them swap,
> bandy, like a flame swerve
> I am their mouth; as a mouth I serve.

It's not as far as you might think from this to bill bissett's "Prayrs for th One Habitation":

> but we all need each othr th
> pebbul th orchard oh th sweet song what
>   takes us joyfully in thru th
>   mercury th passing sea, th flowing
>   salty wave how we touch, touch at
>   th threads of our undrstandings.
>
>   . . .
>
>   ths prayrs with all th rest of it,
>   into the fire, sing, what we
>
>   cum from, what we return to.

APPENDIX ON SNOW:
It is in their attitudes towards winter that Canadians reveal most fully their stance towards Nature – since, as I said at the beginning of this chapter, winter for us is the "real" season.

You can use winter themes and images as a kind of touchstone; collecting snow, ice and blizzards, and different ways of coping with them, can be instructive as well as alarming.

My own collection might begin with Grove's story "Snow" and Lampman's poem "In November." It would certainly include P. K. Page's three stunning poems "The Snowman," "The Skiers" and "Stories of Snow," in all of which the snow takes friendly forms at first but turns during the poem into a metaphor for alienation, terror, manifestation of the inhuman void, and death. It would also contain Alden Nowlan's poem "New Brunswick," which concludes,

> The very dung behind the cattle freezes,
> the wind insults the face like a sprung branch
> who can condemn the exile if he seizes
> an icicle and thrusts it like a lance
>
> into his heart? Oh, Christ our faith is strong
> that winter lasts forever, being long.

It would look at snow used as a death or termination image, as for instance at the end of Ernest Buckler's novel *The Mountain and the Valley* and at the end of Alice Munro's short story "The Time of Death." This use of snow stretches through Graeme Gibson's novel *Five Legs*, with its interminable drive through a snowstorm and its long snowy funeral. (For another funeral in the snow, see Roch Carrier's *La Guerre, Yes Sir!*)

On the positive side, it would include Margaret Avison's "New Year's Poem," in which the "I" looks out from her house, this "unchill, habitable interior," and sees the snow as delightful; and another Avison poem, "Snow." And A. M. Klein's "The Snowshoers," and Jay Macpherson's shepherd-in-the-snow poems in *The Boatman*, in which the snow is not a death-image but the container and preserver of dormant life. And Grove's *Over Prairie Trails*, in which snow and winter are finally accepted on their own terms.

I would end my collection with a quotation from a D. G. Jones poem, "Beating the Bushes: Christmas 1963":

> Shall I curse
> Winter that I do not build a house?
> Shall I hate
> The snow that it is cold?

Nature is a monster, perhaps, only if you come to it with unreal expectations or fight its conditions rather than accepting them and learning to live with them. Snow isn't necessarily something you die in or hate. You can also make houses in it.

Short List:

BIRNEY, Earle, "David," *The Poems of Earle Birney*; NCL, $1.50.
GROVE, F. P., "Snow," WI, $1.95.
MOODIE, Susanna, *Roughing It in the Bush* (condensed); NCL, $1.95.
PRATT, E. J., *Selected Poems*; Macmillan, $1.95.

Long List:

BIRNEY, Earle, "David," *The Poems of Earle Birney*; NCL. Also PMC.
BIRNEY, Earle, "Bushed," *The Poems of Earle Birney*; NCL. Also G&B.
 Also PMC.
BIRNEY, Earle, "Transcontinental," *The Poems of Earle Birney*; NCL.
BISSETT, bill, "Prayrs for th One Habitation," *Nobody Owns th Earth*; AN.
CRAWFORD, Isabella, "Malcolm's Katie," *Nineteenth Century Narrative Poems* (ed. David Sinclair); NCL.

FRYE, Northrop, *The Bush Garden*; AN.

GROVE, F. P., "Snow," W1.

LAYTON, Irving, "The Birth of Tragedy," *Collected Poems*; M&S. Also PMC.

LAYTON, Irving, "For Mao Tse-Tung: A Meditation on Flies and Kings," *Collected Poems*; M&S.

LEE, Dennis, *Civil Elegies*; AN.

LePAN, Douglas, "A Country Without a Mythology," *The Book of Canadian Poetry* (ed. A. J. M. Smith); Gage.

MARSHALL, Joyce, "The Old Woman," W1.

McLACHLAN, Alexander, "The Emigrant," *The Book of Canadian Poetry* (ed. A. J. M. Smith); Gage.

MOODIE, Susanna, *Roughing It in the Bush* (condensed); NCL.

NOWLAN, Alden, "April in New Brunswick," *Under the Ice*; R, OP.

PRATT, E. J., "The Titanic," *Selected Poems*; Macmillan.

PRATT, E. J., "Towards the Last Spike," *Selected Poems*; Macmillan. Also *Poets Between the Wars* (ed. Milton Wilson); NCL.

ROSS, Sinclair, "The Painted Door," W1.

3

ANIMAL VICTIMS

Have the wild things no moral or legal rights? What right has man to inflict such long and fearful agony on a fellow-creature, simply because that creature does not speak his language?

                             – *Ernest Thompson Seton,*
                                   "Redruff"

The dead beast, turned up
(brown fur on back and white
on the belly), lay on the roadway,
its paws extended in the air –
worn-out attitude of prayer.

It was beautiful on the well-travelled roadway
with its dead black lips: God help me,
I did not even know what it was.
I had been walking into the city then,
early, with my own name in mind.

                               – *John Newlove,*
                    "The Well-Travelled Roadway"

. . . . in any hunt I'm with the quarry. . . .

                           – *Alden Nowlan,*
      "A Night Hawk Fell With a Sound Like a Shudder"

O the animals we have flayed
to clothe ourselves I poke among,
The rotting carcasses in a shallow pit.
I am looking for one that saved me.

– Stuart MacKinnon,
"On the Way to the Vivarium"

The losers and failures
who never do anything right

. . . . .

who carve in their own image
of maimed animals. . . .

– Al Purdy,
"The Sculptors"

"Do you know why I asked for a dog like Queenie? I did you
know, I especially asked for a poor little handicapped dog that
nobody wanted. . . ."

– Graeme Gibson,
Five Legs

You'd think that the view of Nature as Monster so prevalent in Canadian literature would generate, as the typical Canadian animal story, a whole series of hair-raising tales about people being gnawed by bears, gored to death by evil-eyed moose, and riddled with quills by vengeful porcupines. In fact this is not the case; fangs and claws are sprouted by mountains and icebergs, it's true, but in stories about actual animals something much more peculiar happens, and it's this really odd pattern I'd like to pursue in this chapter. In the course of the hunt I hope to demonstrate that the "realistic" animal story, as invented and developed by Ernest Thompson Seton and Sir Charles G. D. Roberts, is not, as Alec Lucas would have it in *A Literary History of Canada*, "a rather isolated and minor kind of literature," but a *genre* which provides a key to an important facet of the Canadian psyche. Those looking for something "distinctively Canadian" in literature might well start right here.

The Canadian *genre* and its approach to its subject are in fact unique. It is true that stories ostensibly about animals appear in British literature; but as anyone who has read Kipling's Mowgli stories, Kenneth Grahame's *The Wind in the Willows*, or Beatrix Potter's tales can see, the animals in them are really, like the white rabbit in *Alice in Wonderland*, Englishmen in furry zippered suits, often with a layer of human clothing added on top. They speak fluent English and are assigned places in a hierarchical social order which is essentially British (or British-colonial; as in the Mowgli stories): Toad of Toad Hall is an upper-class twit, the stoats and ferrets which invade his mansion are working-class louts and scoundrels. The ease with which these books can be – and have been – translated into plays, ballets and cartoon movies, complete with, song, dance, speech and costume, is an indication of the essentially

73

human nature of the protagonists. Of note also are the invariably happy endings.

Animals appear in American literature minus clothes and the ability to speak English, but seldom are they the centre of the action. Rather they are its goal, as these "animal stories" are in fact hunting stories, with the interest centred squarely on the hunter. The white whale in *Moby-Dick*, the bear in Faulkner's "The Bear," the lion in Hemingway's "The Short Happy Life of Francis Macomber," the grizzlies in Mailer's *Why Are We In Viet Nam?*, the deer glimpsed by the narrator in James Dickey's *Deliverance* – all these and a host of others are animals endowed with magic symbolic qualities. They are Nature, mystery, challenge, otherness, what lies beyond the Frontier: the hunter wishes to match himself against them, conquer them by killing them and assimilate their magic qualities, including their energy, violence and wildness, thus "winning" over Nature and enhancing his own stature. American animal stories are quest stories – with the Holy Grail being a death – usually successful from the hunter's point of view, though not from the animal's; as such they are a comment on the general imperialism of the American cast of mind. When Americans have produced stories which superficially resemble those of Seton and Roberts, they are likely to be animal success-stories, the success being measured in terms of the animal's adjustment to people – as in Jack London's *White Fang*, where the wolf-dog, mistreated in youth, begins by hating men but ends up loving them, saving them and living in California.

The animal stories of Seton and Roberts are far from being success stories. They are almost invariably failure stories, ending with the death of the animal; but this death, far from being the accomplishment of a quest, to be greeted with rejoicing, is seen as tragic or pathetic, *because the stories are told from the point of view of the animal.* That's the key: English animal stories are about "social relations," American ones are about people killing animals; Canadian ones are about animals *being* killed, as felt emotionally from inside the fur and feathers. As you can see, *Moby-Dick* as told by the White Whale would be very different. ("Why is that strange man chasing me around with a harpoon?") For a Canadian version of whale-meets-whaler, see E. J. Pratt's *The Cachalot*, in which it's the whale's death – not the whaler's – that we mourn. (The whaler, incidentally, is from New England. . . .)

"The fact that these stories are true is the reason why all are tragic. The life of a wild animal *always has a tragic end,*" says Seton in the Preface to *Wild Animals I Have Known*. He's defending his position as a realist, a purveyor of truth. However, "realism" in connection with animal stories must always be a somewhat false claim, for the simple reason that animals do not speak a human language; nor do they write stories. It's impossible to get the real inside story, from the horse's mouth so to speak. "Animal" stories must be stories written by people *about* animals, just as "Indian" stories have until very recently been stories written by white people *about* Indians. In the latter case the Indian tends to be made into a symbol; onto him the white man projects his own desire or fear. And so with the animal. "We and the beasts are kin," says Seton, all but acknowledging this connection.

The world of Nature presented by Seton and Roberts is one in which the animal is always a victim. No matter how brave, cunning and strong he is, he will be killed eventually, either by other animals (which these authors don't seem to mind too much; it's part of the game) or by men. Seton, especially, reverses the Nature-as-Monster pattern in stories such as "Lobo," "The Springfield Fox" and "Redruff." Here it is

75

man who is the threat and the villain: the animals suffer much more through men, with their snares, traps, chains and poisons, than they would through other animals, who are at least quick. The amount of elegiac emotion expended over the furry corpses that litter the pages of Seton and Roberts suggest that "tragic" is the wrong word; "pathetic" would be a better one. Tragedy requires a flaw of some kind on the part of the hero, but pathos as a literary mode simply demands that an innocent victim suffer. Seton and Roberts rarely offer their victims even a potential way out. As James Polk says in his essay "Lives of the Hunted: The Canadian Animal Story and the National Identity,"

> These doleful endings and the number of stoic moose, tragic bears, grouse dying in the snow, woodchucks devoured, salmon failing to make it upstream, grief-stricken wolves and doomed balls of fur, feathers or quills squealing for dead mothers tend to instill a certain fatal-ism in the reader. . . .

If animals in literature are always symbols, and if Canadian animal stories present animals as victims, what trait in our national psyche do these animal victims symbolize? By now that should be an easily-guessed riddle, but before unravelling it more fully let's consider two later examples of the realistic animal story as *genre*.

Though Lucas claims that "Nature writing, particularly the animal story, had its heyday in the late nineteenth and early twen-tieth centuries" and has "long passed," two widely-read books have appeared since then which refute him: Fred Bodsworth's *The Last of the Curlews* and Farley Mowat's *Never Cry Wolf*. In Bodsworth's novel the central characters are two birds, the last pair of their species. The book follows them through a season of their life; at its end the female curlew is shot by a man with a gun and the male curlew is left alone. Mowat's book is ostensibly a true-life account of the author's study of a pair of Arctic wolves. The wolves, seen at first as savage predators, emerge as highly commendable beings. But they too are doomed; in an epilogue the author tells us that soon after his visit a Predator Control Officer planted the wolves' den with cyanide, presumably finishing them off.

The difference between the earlier Seton and Roberts stories and the later Bodsworth and Mowat ones is that in the former it is the individual only who dies; the species remains. But *The Last of the Curlews* is, as its name implies, the story of the death of a species, and Mowat indicates that not just the wolves but also the caribou and with them the whole Arctic ecological balance is threatened by the white man's short-sighted and destructive policies. Man is again the villain, but on a much larger scale.

The Canadian concern with doomed and slaughtered animals spreads far beyond the range of the "animal story," however. It is highly visible in poetry, and there's even a recent anthology of "animal poems." Both the title – *The Broken Ark* – and the jacket copy reveal editor Michael Ondaatje's stance, which is firmly in the tradition of Seton and Roberts:

> These are poems that look at animals from the inside out – not the other way round. We don't want to classify them or treat them as pets. We want you to imagine yourself pregnant and being chased and pounded to death by snowmobiles. We want you to feel the cage, and the skin and fur on your shoulders.

In fact, some of the poems in the book aren't this drastic; one is about walking the dog, one about bees, one about happy elephants. But the majority are in what we seem to have identified as the Canadian tradition: the animals in them are dead or dying, their deaths usually caused by man. In Alden Nowlan's "The Bull Moose," the moose is tortured before being killed; the imagery used of him makes him into a sacrificed-god figure, but his is a sacrifice that redeems no one. Irving Layton's "Cain" is a meditation on a frog he has himself killed with an air-rifle; presumably the title makes the frog his brother. Pat Lane's "Mountain Oysters" tells about the routine castration of rams; in bill bissett's "Killer Whale" the whales have been captured and will obviously die. In each case we are asked to sympathize with the animals, not with the men who are torturing or killing them.

There are many others that *The Broken Ark* misses. Prominent among them are Irving Layton's "The Bull Calf," in which the animal, like Nowlan's moose, is being sacrificed uselessly. Then there's Al Purdy's extraordinary poem "The Death of Animals," in which animal deaths and trivial human activities are juxtaposed, with the human activities seen as causal (though the poet claims, ironically, that there is "no connection"): the humans are taking over, replacing the animals:

> Fox in deep burrow suddenly imagined
> a naked woman inside his rubric fur,
> lacquered fingernails pushing, edging him out:
> . and screamed, directly into the earth.

And castration again, in Alden Nowlan's "God Sour the Milk of the Knacking Wench."

Turning to recent prose fiction, we find the animal as victim making a significant appearance in the work of Dave Godfrey. *Death Goes Better with Coca-Cola*, Godfrey's first book, is essentially a collection of hunting stories. The point is made partly by the title, which links death with coca-cola, the great American beverage; partly by the initial quote, which is from biologist Konrad Lorenz's book *On Aggression* and which speaks of the destructive effect cultures regarded as "higher" – "as the culture of a conquering nation usually is" – have on those on "the subdued side"; and partly by the first story, "The Generation of Hunters," which is about a boy who is taught by his father how to shoot bears and who grows up to be a Marine. Americans, "the conquering nation," are the killers, Canadians are the killed, as the last story, "The Hard-Headed Collector," makes clear. The slaughter of moose and fish which occurs elsewhere in the stories, and which is performed in some cases by Canadians, is thus given an ironic framework: Canadians too can be hunters, but only by taking a stance towards Nature which is like the stance of America towards them. The only "authentic" hunters are those who must still kill to eat, the Indians and locals who "really live here." The rest are fakes, memento hunters, as the man who sets out to catch a flying fish in "The Flying Fish" learns when the fish he is allowed to hook turns out to be made of polyfoam. "It is something to mount on my wall," he says.

There's a fascinating poem by Alden Nowlan called "Hunters" which takes Americans-as-hunters a step further. The hunters, "Americans in scarlet breeches," have shot a bear which is roped to their car; one of them gets out to check the knots, looking "boyish," and Nowlan comments,

> . . . One senses how this cowed
> and squalid beast enlivens him – its pain
> and cornered anger squelched in the dark wood
> that ornaments his world. It's like a child
> sprung from the violent act but tamed and good,
> decoratively. . . .

The Americans have been performing their ritual act of "taming" Nature by killing one of its animals, but somehow the thing is no longer real; the dark wood is now just ornamental, the dead animal a decoration, not something that can be seen as itself:

> . . . He can't see it wild,
> alive in its own element. He might
> as well have bought it and perhaps he did:
> guides trap and sell them out by weight
> to hunters who don't want to hunt. The dead
> beast-thing secured, the car starts homeward. There
> bear skins are rugs, a den is not a lair.

Canada and America have interesting roles in this poem. America's hunter-energy is running down, though a dead animal can still produce an enlivening thrill. Canada is the place where Americans now come to hunt. The dead bear is Canadian, a trophy to be taken from "here" to "there," and "there" is seen as civilized, safe, non-wild, a place of rituals that have lost their meaning and of fake surfaces, of living skins turned into rugs. The function of the Canadian "guides" is curious; they are the middlemen, converting their own live reality to dead trophies so they can sell it. The narrative stance hovers tantalizingly between sympathy for the bear and potential fear of it; at any rate, the bear is real for the narrator in a way that it is not for the Americans.

We've established that the animal as victim is a persistent image in Canadian literature; now here's a further clue to its possible meaning. Biologist Desmond Morris conducted a survey of people's reactions to animals, through which he made the not surprising discovery that the animals people choose to identify with depend on the size and age of the people.

Small children like large "parental" animals such as bears and elephants; slightly older children prefer white mice and squirrels and other things smaller than themselves which they can control; adolescents like companion or sexual-power figures such as dogs and horses; childless couples tend to favour substitute children such as cats, lapdogs and housebirds. Very rarely is an animal liked or disliked for itself alone; it is chosen for its symbolic anthropomorphic values.

Elderly people in England tended to identify with threatened or nearly-extinct species; obviously they themselves felt threatened or nearly-extinct. But in Canada it is the nation as a whole that joins in animal-salvation campaigns such as the protest over the slaughter of baby seals and the movement to protect the wolf. This could – mistakenly, I think – be seen as national guilt: Canada after all was founded on the fur trade, and an animal cannot painlessly be separated from its skin. From the animal point of view, Canadians are as bad as the slave trade or the Inquisition; which casts a new light on those beavers on the nickels and caribou on the quarters. But it is much more likely that Canadians themselves feel threatened and nearly-extinct as a nation, and suffer also from life-denying experience as individuals – the culture threatens the "animal" within them – and that their identification with animals is the expression of a deep-seated cultural fear. The animals, as Seton says, are us. And for the Canadian animal, bare survival is the main aim in life, failure as an individual is inevitable, and extinction as a species is a distinct possibility.

A search for animal victims in Québec literature uncovers an interesting phenomenon: the "realistic" version of the animal victim is almost unknown. Animals, when they appear, are more likely to be Aesop-fable humanoids like the bull in Jacques Ferron's story "Mélie and the Bull." The explanation may lie in the persistence of the French fable tradition in Québec; or it may be that French Canadians have been more than willing to see themselves as victims, conquered and exploited, while English Canadians suppressed this knowledge of themselves – they won on the Plains of Abraham, didn't they? – and were able to project it only through their use of animal images.

However, there is one encounter with an animal in French Canadian literature which could be straight out of Ernest Thompson Seton: I'm thinking of the moment in Gabrielle Roy's *The Hidden Mountain* where Pierre, having hunted down a caribou, finally kills it and it turns upon him a gaze full of resignation and suffering. This gaze exchanged between a hunter and an animal either dying or threatened with death – and it's usually a deer, moose or caribou – is a recurring moment in Canadian literature; in it the hunter identifies with his prey *as suffering victim*. For an example from Seton, see *The Trail of the Sandhill Stag*, in which the narrator finally corners a stag after a long hunt but can't shoot because – during that meaningful gaze – he realizes that the stag is his brother.

In *The Bush Garden*, Northrop Frye notes "the prevalence in Canada of animal stories, in which animals are closely assimilated to human behaviour and emotions." I would add that the human behaviour and emotions in question are limited in range, being usually flight, fear and pain. Applying Morris' findings, we may infer that the English Canadian projects himself through his animal images as a threatened victim, confronted by a superior alien technology against which he feels powerless, unable to take any positive defensive action, and, survive each crisis as he may, ultimately doomed.

———◇———

This is not to say that one shouldn't be humane towards

animals or protect the wolf; one should, though in saying so I may simply be demonstrating my own Canadianism. But there comes a point at which seeing yourself as a victimized animal – naming your condition, as the crucial step from the ignorance of Position One through the knowledge of Position Two to the self-respect of Position Three – can become the *need* to see yourself as a victimized animal, and at that point you will be locked into Position Two, unable to go any further. This insight is explored with ruthless precision in Graeme Gibson's two novels, *Five Legs* and *Communion*. The central organizing images in both books are animal images, and the use Gibson makes of them pulls together everything I've said so far about animal victims in Canadian literature.

The title of the first novel, *Five Legs*, refers to a mutant water-buffalo which a nasty woman at a funeral in Southern Ontario has seen in a Mexican zoo. The animal has five legs instead of four, and because of its deformity people are laughing and throwing stones at it. The woman has vowed to become a collector of warped animals, and has already managed to locate a dog with three legs; she is currently looking for a deformed cat. She latches on to one of the novel's two protagonists, Felix Oswald, and her interest in him – he realizes with horror – is of the same kind: she sees him as a cripple, a victim and a freak. She's very perceptive, since this is in fact how he sees himself. The woman's pathological need to seek out victims is matched by Felix's pathological need to be one.

Later Felix changes the emphasis slightly: instead of a caged mutant, he has a fantasy of himself as a free wild animal, a moose. In the fantasy the moose is in flight from a group of pursuers, from which it is only barely managing to escape. (It's significant that Felix has acquired his moose image from the drunken monologue of a pitiful loser, who in the first section of the book is rambling on both about a moose he has allowed to

83

get away and a deer he has shot and now feels remorseful about.)

The moose image is picked up in a later conversation, this time a discussion about hunting. There are two "sides" in the discussion: one taken by a group of conventional businessmen who emphasize the joys of the kill – "By George that's a, a satisfying feeling!" – and the other taken by Max, an eccentric old bohemian, who says he'd never shoot a moose or "any other of the round earth's living creatures" and goes on to tell, stealing his metaphors from the drunken driver in section one, how he once saw a moose "stumbling on the shore and rushing to the bush like a man in flames," and how when it looked at him it had "tears of blood in the eyes' dark corners." (There's that sacrificial victim imagery again, and the exchange of gazes between hunter and prey.) An American would have pulled the trigger, and in fact the men turn on Max, accuse him of being a subversive, claim that hunting is "the very BASIS of our social fabric," insist that they are successful because "We know how to get things done," and extend their assumed usefulness even further: "we're hunters, that's right . . . The community needs people like us. The country . . . . whole free world!" These "practical" men are, it appears, not only capitalists but internationalists too; like the hunters in Godfrey's stories, they hunt for symbolic reasons, not because they need the dead animals for food.

Putting Gibson's patterns together, we find two sorts of people: those who are successful by "international" (or American) society's proclaimed standards, who are identified as hunters, soldiers, and aggressive moneymen; and those who are failures – the drunken driver, Max and Felix – who express sympathy with hunted animals and refuse to kill them. Felix, in fact, *is* an animal, a victim in flight; the "hunters," the forces of society, are in pursuit, and will capture and kill him if they can. No positive action, no defence, is possible for him; he can only run away – as he does, literally, at the end of the novel.

Even though he is running *away*, not towards anything, Felix does escape in *Five Legs*. But we know from Seton that animal stories – Canadian ones at least – always have a tragic end, and in *Communion* Gibson corrects any mistaken impression we might have had that Felix's escape could ever have been anything but temporary. Again, it is Felix's *need* to be a hunted animal that does it; his condition, though it is partly a reflection of his environment, seems as much willed as imposed. In *Communion* Gibson pushes the animal-victim identification as far as it can go: if you are determined to be a victim, that's exactly what you will be.

In *Communion* Felix is still in flight, but now he is escaping not only from society but from all human emotions and involvements, including sexual ones. He is in love with two stone statues in a cemetery, and he feels more for the diseased animals at the veterinarian's where he works than he does for anyone else. He singles out one particular animal, a sick husky dog, which is, like the crippled water buffalo in *Five Legs*, incurable. But whereas the buffalo can live with its deformity (however unpleasantly), the dog is mortally ill. Felix has fantasies of taking the dog out into the winter bush and freeing it, thereby freeing – perhaps – a part of himself, his own trapped and wounded life-energies. But when he acts out this fantasy, stealing the dog and driving it to a spot outside the city, it refuses to leave the car. Like Felix, it is choosing its own entrapment. When he finally manages to pry it loose, it runs along beside his moving car; he hits it by accident and it dies in agony. His attempted act of redemption has failed; but then, had he wanted success, he might have chosen a more redeemable subject.

His second attempted act of redemption fails also. In flight from everything by now, he gets a lift with a sadistic truck-driver and ends up in the United States. In the "Canadian" portion of *Communion*, the life-destroying forces are seen as mainly personal and internal: the paralyzing guilt, the inability to act, the incapacity to respond to authority by anything but flight, the sexual stasis, the sense of placelessness and exile, the lack of contact with any source of true feeling – all these are individual and private, rarely even verbalized. But once across the border the violence and destructiveness that is repressed and turned in upon itself in Canada is seen as external, *there* in the real world, rampantly at large. Ritson, the "American" character in *Communion*, is another hunted animal, but this time his condition is literal: he lives in a cellar, comes out at night to scrounge for food, and fights with other people who are also animals; the American city is the new locale, apparently, for Darwinian marginal survival. In America people-as-animals are not just victims, they are savage cornered beasts.

Felix dies trying to save his American *alter ego* from being burned up by a nightmarish group of children. In his attempt to stop the children he kills one of them and – as when he killed the dog by accident – he is so overcome with horror by the image of himself as predator rather than victim that he is paralyzed. Ritson escapes and Felix burns in his stead – ironically, since the life he has saved is scarcely human.

What Gibson has done in his two books is to take the naming of the condition a step further. Perhaps our condition is that of "exploited victim," but by now our *real* condition may be "those who *need* to be exploited victims." That's a tougher condition; the first could be changed by altering the external environment, but the second also involves the alteration of self, of the way we see ourselves. Felix's sexual, emotional and practical paralyses are all correlatives of never having accepted any role but that of victim.

———◦———

I promised a ray of light at the end of each chapter, but for this one it isn't easy. However.

For other uses of animal images, you might try looking at some of Michael Ondaatje's animal poems. The aggressor-victim thing is still going on, but in Ondaatje the animal is more likely to incorporate a vitality and energy (which man finds threatening) than to be a suffering victim. Or you could look at Joe Rosenblatt's book *Bumblebee Dithyramb*, which has a number of animal poems in it. Rosenblatt also sees animals as centres of irrepressible vitality, though it sometimes seems as though he can approach this kind of vitality *only* through animals – it is somehow closed to man. Through his highly-charged use of language the animals can do and become things for him that human beings can't; they are surrogates for desire rather than for fear.

I'd like to end by looking at another Layton poem, "A Tall Man Executes A Jig." This is an astonishing poem, and it becomes even more astonishing when read in the light of everything I've said about animal victims. In it, the tall man proceeds through various meditations in a field full of purposeless gnats. He moves out of the field and stands waiting for a revelation, and what he gets is a revelation that is also a "temptation": he sees "A violated grass snake that lugs / Its intestine like a small red valise." It's his reaction that's the astonishment:

And the man wept because pity was useless.
"Your jig's up; the flies come like kites," he said

87

And watched the grass snake crawl towards the hedge,
Convulsing and dragging into the dark
The satchel filled with curses for the earth,
For the odours of warm sedge, and the sun,
A blood-red organ in the dying sky.
Backwards it fell into a grassy ditch,
Exposing its underside, white as milk,
And mocked by wisps of hay between its jaws;
And then it stiffened to its final length.
But though it opened its thin mouth to scream
A last silent scream that shook the black sky,
Adamant and fierce, the tall man did not curse.

The temptation for the tall man would have been to see himself as the suffering and dying snake, "violated" and victimized, to see life as death, to see the only appropriate response as a hopeless cursing of all that is. What makes the tall man tall is that he resists temptation: he witnesses the suffering but he does not curse. Considering the almost overwhelming pressures of the great Canadian animal-victim tradition, this restraint is heroic.

Short List:

BODSWORTH, Fred, *The Last of the Curlews*; NCL, $1.95.
GIBSON, Graeme, *Communion*; AN, $2.50.
MOWAT, Farley, *Never Cry Wolf*; Dell, $0.95.
ROBERTS, Charles G. D., *The Last Barrier*; NCL, $1.95.
SETON, Ernest Thompson, *Wild Animals I Have Known*; Schocken Books, $2.95.

Long List:

BODSWORTH, Fred, *The Last of the Curlews*; NCL.

FERRON, Jacques, "Mélie and the Bull," *Tales From the Uncertain Country*; AN.

GIBSON, Graeme, *Communion*; AN.

GIBSON, Graeme, *Five Legs*; AN.

GODFREY, David, *Death Goes Better With Coca-Cola*; Press Porcépic.

LAYTON, Irving, "A Tall Man Executes a Jig," *Collected Poems*; M&S. Also G&B. Also PMC.

LAYTON, Irving, "The Bull Calf," *Collected Poems*; M&S.

LUCAS, Alec, *A Literary History of Canada* (ed. Carl Klinck); UTP.

MOWAT, Farley, *Never Cry Wolf*; Dell.

NOWLAN, Alden, "God Sour the Milk of the Knacking Wench," *Under the Ice*; R. OP. Also G&B. Also PMC.

ONDAATJE, Michael, ed., *The Broken Ark*; Oberon.

POLK, James, "Lives of the Hunted: The Canadian Animal Story and the National Identity," *Canadian Literature*, Summer 1972.

PRATT, E. J., "The Cachalot," *Selected Poems*; Macmillan.

PURDY, Al, "The Death of Animals," *Poems for All the Annettes*; AN, OP.

ROBERTS, Charles G. D., *The Last Barrier*; NCL.

ROSENBLATT, Joe, *Bumblebee Dithyramb*; Press Porcépic. Also ML.

SETON, Ernest Thompson, *Wild Animals I Have Known*; Schocken Books.

4

FIRST PEOPLE
Indians and Eskimos as Symbols

. . . There lived a soul more wild than barbarous;
A tameless soul – the sunburnt savage free –
Free, and untainted by the greed of gain:
Great Nature's man content with Nature's good.

– *Charles Mair*,
Tecumseh

Before the year was gone the priests were shown
The way the Hurons could prepare for death
A captive foe. The warriors had surprised
A band of Iroquois and had reserved
the one survivor for a fiery pageant.
No cunning of an ancient Roman triumph,
Nor torment of a Medici confession
Surpassed the subtle savagery of art
which made the dressing for the sacrifice
A ritual of mockery for the victim.

– *E. J. Pratt*,
Brébeuf and His Brethren

When *Brébeuf and His Brethren* first came out, a friend of mine
said that the thing to do now was to write the same story from
the Iroquois point of view.

– *James Reaney*,
"The Canadian Poet's Predicament"

Their past is sold in a shop: the beaded shoes,
the sweetgrass basket, the curio Indian,
burnt wood and gaudy cloth and inch-canoes –
trophies and scalpings for a traveller's den.
Sometimes, it's true, they dance, but for a bribe;
after a deal don the bedraggled feather
and welcome a white mayor to the tribe.

– *A. M. Klein,*
"Indian Reservation: Caughnawaga"

When we go into the Rockies we may have the sense that gods
are there. But if so, they cannot manifest themselves to us as
ours. They are the gods of another race, and we cannot know
them because of what we are, and what we did.

– *George Grant,*
Technology and Empire

My interest in this pack of failures betrays my character.
– *Leonard Cohen,*
Beautiful Losers

Until very recently, Indians and Eskimos made their only appearances in Canadian literature in books written by white writers. Thus the position of the writer in relation to the Indians and Eskimos has been much the same as his position in relation to the animals in animal stories: an imported white man looks at a form of natural or native life alien to himself and appropriates it for symbolic purposes. The Indians and Eskimos have rarely been considered in and for themselves; they are usually made into projections of something in the white Canadian psyche, a fear or a wish.

In American literature there are two traditional ways of approaching the Indian. (The Eskimo, for obvious geographical reasons, is scarcely present.) One is the idealization of the Indian as a Noble Savage *à la Rousseau*, represented most obviously by Chingachgook in Fenimore Cooper's Leatherstocking romances. Here the Indian is more primitive than the white man, closer to Nature, and therefore closer to certain instincts and moral values that the white man has lost: courage, loyalty, the ability to relate to his surroundings, and so forth. The other tradition is that of the Indian as inferior (see, for instance, the ugly, dirty Indians in Francis Parkman's *The Oregon Trail*) or as evil, like Indian Joe in *Tom Sawyer* and the Indians Chillingworth consorts with in Hawthorne's *The Scarlet Letter*. Cooper too has bad Indians, usually Iroquois, and no act of violence or depravity is beyond them. It is perhaps significant that his "good" Indian, Chingachgook, belongs to a nearly extinct tribe: he and his son are the *last* of the Mohicans. The Indians can be idealized only when they're about to vanish.

Of course, the values ascribed to the Indian will depend on what the white writer feels about Nature, and America has always had mixed feelings about that. At one end of the spectrum is Thoreau, wishing to immerse himself in swamps for the positive vibrations; at the other end is Benjamin Franklin, who didn't like Nature. He thought it was unfortunate that the Indians got so drunk on the white man's firewater, but maybe it was a good thing after all because that way they would die sooner and make way for Civilization. Most Western movies are on the side of Franklin: the usual happy ending is the defeat of the Indian.

Canada has a dual literary tradition for Indians too, but as you might expect it isn't Good Guy/Bad Guy but Victor/Victim. The distinction is worth making. American Good Guy Indians are admirable, but they are not necessarily persecuted by whites. Bad Guy Indians are depicted as a threat, but they don't necessarily win the frontier wars. On the contrary they lose, *because* they have been defined as evil. However, the point about Canadian Indians as Victors is not that they are thoroughly evil, but that they torture and kill whites, with whom the author identifies. And the point about Indians as Victims is not that they are good or superior, but that they are persecuted. The Americans, then, go for moral definitions based on intrinsic qualities the Indians are thought to possess; a rather racist approach. The Canadians, on the other hand, zero in on the relative places of Indians and whites on the aggression-suffering scale. Please note that none of this need have much to do with how Americans and Canadians treated Indians *historically*. (Canadians in fact have a slightly better track record.) What we are looking at are the different patterns of image and symbol that the two countries have made from their encounter with the first inhabitants of this continent.

Charles Mair's verse drama *Tecumseh* is roughly the equivalent in the "Indian" sphere of attempted Divine-Mother writings in the Nature sphere: the Indian is seen as one of Nature's children, living a jolly carefree life until the advent of the white man. Even here, though, the Indian-as-victim motif begins to surface. But the main emphasis in Tecumseh's speeches is on the peacefulness and good behaviour of the Indian. In the same vein is Joseph Howe's "Song of the Micmac," in which the Indians come through as Walter Scott warrior heroes. The juxtaposition of European mode and Canadian content produces some deliriously cross-eyed effects:

> Oh! who on the mountain, the plain, or the wave,
>> With the arm of the Micmac will dare to contend?
> Who can hurl the keen spear with the sons of the brave
>> Or who can the bow with such energy bend?

> Who can follow the Moose, or the wild Cariboo,
>> With a footstep as light and unwearied as he?
> Who can bring down the Loon with an arrow so true,
>> Or paddle his bark o'er as stormy a sea?
> . . . .
> Free sons of the forest, then peal forth the song,
>> Till each valley and rock shall of victory tell,
> And the ghosts of our heroes, while flitting along,
>> With triumph shall smile on the spots where they fell.

But such renderings of gleeful activity and harmless pranks soon give way to a version of the Indian which is less innocent and more threatening: the Indian as tormentor. The Indian as the Victor half of a pattern in which the white man plays the Victim is of course related to the Nature-as-Monster complex. This stance is epitomized by E. J. Pratt's long narrative poem, *Brébeuf and His Brethren*. In a sense *Brébeuf* is the all-Canadian poem: it's about a French Catholic priest killed by Indians, as seen by a white English-speaking Protestant Canadian from

97

Newfoundland. Nature for Pratt is consistently destructive; thus man's task is not to identify with Nature but to oppose it, and Pratt opposes it with an ordered human society which embodies the virtues of courage, dedication, love and sacrifice. Whether you think the Jesuit mission to convert the Indians really did exemplify these virtues is beside the point: that is how the Jesuits are seen by the poem. The Indians, being on the side of Nature, are made to represent the senseless destructiveness, cruelty and violence which can be seen also in Pratt's hurricanes and icebergs. As Northrop Frye says in *The Bush Garden*, ". . . the mutilation and destruction of the gigantic Brébeuf and the other missionaries is a sacrificial rite in which the Indians represent humanity in the state of Nature and are agents of its unconscious barbarity."

Thus Pratt dwells consistently not only on the more disagreeable aspects of Nature but on those of the Indians as well. No blue skies and stately trees for Brébeuf. His experience of the Canadian wilderness is like a city-dweller's nightmare of a canoe trip; it is one

> Of rocks and cataracts and portages,
> Of feet cut by the river stones, of mud
> And stench, of boulders, logs and tangled growths,
> Of summer heat that made him long for night,
> And when he struck his bed of rock – mosquitoes
> That made him doubt if dawn would never break.

Similarly the Indians, even the ones initially friendly or at least tolerant of him, are far from being Noble Savages. The description of life with them reads like a cross between a slum-clearance proposal and an antacid ad:

. . . the martyrdom of smoke
That hourly drove his nostrils to the ground
To breathe, or offered him the choice of death
Outside by frost, inside by suffocation;
The forced companionship of dogs that ate
From the same platters, slept upon his legs
Or neck; the nausea from sagamite,
Unsalted, gritty, and that bloated feeling. . . .

The medicine men are corrupt and malicious, the warriors are sadistic, the "reeking children" and the squaws have fleas.

The typical American "Indian story" relates the clash of two opposing cultures along an advancing line known as the Frontier. The whites advance, fight and win, conquering the territory as they go, the Indians lose and retreat, and this state of affairs is seen as proper. In Pratt's "Indian story" – and in similar stories in which the Indians are part of Nature the Monster – there is no frontier and no white civilization advancing in a vertical straight line across the continent. Instead the white expedition is small and totally surrounded by enemy territory, and the Indians win.

Brébeuf's trip takes him into a wilderness that engulfs him and an alien society with which he must at first pretend to merge. Inside the wilderness but disapproving of it and of Indian society, he eventually constructs his garrison, a four-square structure enclosed by walls, with a separate enclosure for tame Indians. He has built a shell for himself: outside the walls are the hostile forces, Nature and the Indians; inside them are the Christianity and the French civilization Brébeuf has imported. (For a similar "garrison" in the work of an earlier writer, see John Richardson's romance *Wacousta*.) Brébeuf's goal is to expand the wall so that finally all the Indians will be inside it, converts to Catholicism and French. The Hurons later see him as the Evil One, and from their point of view – though not from Pratt's – he is.

Unless your aim is conversion, the making of Canada into an imitation Europe and of the Indians into imitation Europeans, the fear of Nature projected in *Brébeuf* is not the only available attitude. Brébeuf in effect refuses to accept the land as it is, and it destroys him; but one may travel in a strange country not to convert but to explore or to observe. The position then taken will be, ostensibly at least, not a hostile one but a neutral one; and such neutrality has become possible for more recent writers. The writer-as-observer appears for instance in Al Purdy's sequence of journalistic poems, *North of Summer*, in which the Eskimos Purdy finds himself among are viewed neither as "good" nor as "bad" but as simply other. Insofar as Purdy allows them to symbolize anything – and he has a habit of undercutting his own symbolism – they embody a primitive civilization which is being trivialized by the gimmicks of white culture.

But lurking beneath neutrality for Canadian writers is the ever-present victim motif, and it surfaces in three other Purdy poems, "Lament For The Dorsets," "Beothuk Indian Skeleton in a Glass Case," and "Remains of an Indian Village," elegies each of them for extinct peoples. The first two take as their subjects races of vanished giants who couldn't compete with "little men" and whites, the third a village wiped out by disease. Eskimos in the flesh Purdy finds alien and difficult to communicate or identify with (except, of course, the carvers whose work is rejected or broken, the old men, and so forth). It is natives who are dead or extinct that really say something to him, give him a meaningful reflection of himself; it is these whose "broken consonants" he can hear.

Another writer who begins with neutral observation and arrives at identification is Farley Mowat in *The People of the*

Deer. Again, it is the threatened and eventually doomed position of the group he chooses that seems to make identification possible for him. Ostensibly a true-life narrative of the decline and fall of a tribe of Barren Lands Eskimo, whose staple was caribou and who starved to death when the caribou population declined, the book is actually a prose elegy on a vanishing race, a race destroyed by the intrusion of a technologically "superior" race whose values it adopts but which are unsuited to the land. Mowat's Arctic, like Purdy's, is littered with relics and artefacts of earlier, even more extinct civilizations: bones, stone tent rings, lost carvings. One anecdote in the book which achieves mythic proportions is the story of the shaman's son who becomes obsessed with the white man's powers, makes a long journey to the nearest trading post from which he brings back not only a pile of worthless gadgets – gramophone, pots, bric à brac – but a disease which devastates his tribe. By the time Mowat sees him he is a miserly old man, living in isolation and surrounded by the rusting pieces of junk he has collected, symbols of the white man's ways which are at best useless and at worst deadly. But junk isn't the only thing he's imported: he's also imported the white man's Victor/Victim categories. Made a victim himself by his internalization of white greed, he has returned to victimize the other members of his tribe by terrorism and intimidation.

But the whole tribe is fated, and ultimately all its members die. Mowat looks, empathizes and finds himself able to do nothing; or nothing that works. He can define the problem but he can't solve it. The book might well have been called *Lament For A Nation*.

An earlier book which approaches the dying native culture from a somewhat different angle is Emily Carr's *Klee Wyck*. This is a collection of deceptively understated small prose sketches drawn from a painter's experiences among West Coast

Indians. As in *North of Summer* and *People of the Deer*, the white protagonist immerses herself in the forest and the alien people, returning to tell the story. Again we have the artefacts, abandoned and decaying; in this case the rotting totem poles with their gigantic animal shapes. Again we have the enveloping, faintly threatening environment, not the freezing North this time but the lush and impenetrable British Columbia rain forests. The Indians, however, are not extinct; they have merely declined, and although the causes are not explicitly set forth they are there in the sharply drawn details of the sketches: the missionary teachers, imposing on the Indian children a culture they have no interest in learning and which will accomplish nothing for them; the priests; the ever-present Hudson's Bay posts. The results are there too: the squalor, the indifference, the unfinished houses, the pidgin English the Indians are forced to use when speaking with the whites. Most memorably, the Indian mothers whose babies die with predictable regularity and are buried one after another in the Indian cemeteries.

Carr's Indians still have, in their neglected totem poles, a visible reminder of a vanished but surely preferable past. When even this has disappeared the Indian emerges in Canadian literature as the ultimate victim of social oppression and deprivation. The Blacks fill this unenviable role in American literature, but Canadians, though they have a few Black ghettoes of their own, are reluctant to write about them. In American literature the Indian, whether Good Guy or Bad Guy, is always somehow outside white civilization, whereas the Black is inside it; witness the difference between Indian Joe in *Tom Sawyer*, a lurker on the outskirts, and the domestic Nigger Jim in *Huckleberry Finn*. Or the difference between Faulkner's Dilsey of *The Sound and the Fury* and Sam Fathers of "The Bear": the former is the sustainer of the white family she works for, the latter, despite his name, not one of the family at all but a source of alien, primitive and arcane knowledge. In Canadian literature the place of low man on the totem pole *within* the society is reserved for the Indian.

Two places where the Indian as social victim may be found are George Ryga's play, *The Ecstasy of Rita Joe*, and Margaret Laurence's books, *A Bird in the House* and *The Fire Dwellers*. In Ryga's play the Indian heroine is subjected to every possible form of exploitation – economic, cultural, and sexual – and is finally raped and murdered. Through it all she is passive and helpless, her only recourse evasion or outright flight. Here it is the whites who take the role of aggressive savages: violent and perverted, they stand for the hostility of the entire external universe. There is, it's true, a white judge who tries to help Rita, but because he can do so only on his own terms, which are those of white society – and especially, one feels, because Rita herself is so firmly locked into her role as victim – his help is ineffectual. His speech summarizes the conditions imposed upon the Indian in his social-victim position:

> The cities are open to you and you come and go as you wish, yet you gravitate to the slums and the skid-rows and the shanty-town fringes. You become a whore, drunkard, user of narcotics. . . . At best dying of illness or malnutrition. . . . At worst, kicked or beaten to death by some angry white scum who finds in you something lower than himself to pound his frustrations out on. What's to be done? You Indians seem to be incapable of taking action to help yourselves.

In Margaret Laurence's books, the Indians are represented by the Métis Tonnerre family. The young white girl Vanessa in *A Bird in the House* takes Piquette Tonnerre to her summer cottage, but what the encounter reveals to Vanessa is the enormous gap which separates them. Piquette's subsequent history, as told both in this book and in *The Fire Dwellers*, is distressing: she marries an "Englishman" who abandons her, forcing her to return to the shack of a home she thought she'd escaped. She and her children are burned to death when the house catches fire during one of her drinking bouts. Stacey, the heroine of *The Fire Dwellers*, hears this from Piquette's sister Val, a broken-down streetwalker, old before her time: she is what Rita Joe would have turned into if she'd lived. Stacey can sympathize, but ultimately the spectacle of Indian-as-victim embarrasses her: not only is there nothing she can do to help, but she can't even identify completely. The Indians are too hopeless, despondent and futile, even for her. This is brought out also in a speech made by another character in the book, talking about a remote West Coast village:

> . . . Indian village, a bunch of rundown huts and everything dusty, even the kids and dogs covered with dust like they were all hundreds of years old which maybe they are and dying which they almost certainly are. And they look at you . . . with a sort of inchoate hatred and who could be surprised at it? . . . If I were one of them . . . I'd sure as hell hate people like me, coming in from the outside. . . . You don't ask anybody anything. You haven't suffered enough. You don't know what they know. You don't have the right to pry. So you look, and then you go away.

The Indians are, finally, a yardstick of suffering against which the whites can measure their own and find it lacking: whatever their own miseries, the Indians can do them one better. "Shit,

Stacey, you got worries?" Val asks. "Go ahead – make me laugh."

We might expect some writers to have connected the animal-as-victim motif with the Indian-as-victim one, and this does in fact happen: Indians seen as animals once free, wild and beautiful, now caged, captive and sickly. This metaphor appears in the work of such superficially different writers as Hugh Garner and A. M. Klein, one a "realist," the other an extravagant metaphor-artist. In Klein's poem, "Indian Reservation: Caughnawaga," the pattern is set forth clearly. The Indians of the past are admirable animals:

> Where are the tribes, the feathered bestiaries? –
> Rank Aesop's animals erect and red,
> with fur on their names to make all live things kin –
> Chief Running Deer, Black Bear, Old Buffalo Head?

The poem answers its own question: the animals are where all captured or nearly-extinct animals may be found, in zoos and cages (otherwise known as reservations):

> This is a grassy ghetto, and no home.
> And these are fauna in a museum kept.
> The better hunters have prevailed. The game
> losing its blood, now makes these grounds its crypt.
> The animals pale, the shine of the fur is lost. . . .

In Klein's poem, the relics of the lost primitive past are still in evidence, but as trivialized curios used to extract money from the tourists. Big Tom in Garner's story "One, Two, Three Little Indians" is a similar zoo animal whose Indian past has become for him a degrading mockery. The story begins with Big Tom telling a story himself, a folktale made of "victorious words."

But the story is told to a child too young to understand it, who dies anyway at the end of the story, and Big Tom himself remembers the "old dialect" only imperfectly. He makes money by selling baskets at the side of the road with a feather stuck in his hat: he is forced to play "Indian" to fulfill the expectations of the American tourists, who want local colour. "'I wish he'd look at the camera,'" one of them says, "as though he were talking of an animal in a cage." Tom's "Indian" identity serves only to imprison him yet further: it is what makes the cage.

It's interesting that the tourists are *American*, just as are the hunters in Nowlan's poem "The Hunters." In fact, white Canadian identification with the Indian-as-victim may at times conceal a syllogism something like the following: "We are to the Americans as the Indians are to us." In one of Dave Godfrey's stories, "On the River," the white protagonist lies to an old lady who asks him what he is: "I'm an Indian," he says. It's a joke, but in the context of Godfrey's book (Americans as aggressors), maybe it isn't so funny. Certainly in Yves Thériault's two books, *Agaguk* and *Ashini*, the native heroes are used as more or less thinly-veiled disguises for a presentation of French Canadian problems. *Agaguk* – with its son who rejects his father's inbred and static culture and tries to make it on his own, and the wife who demands certain "mother" rights – concentrates on the internal or domestic situation (though Agaguk is exploited by whites, both "legitimately" through the trading company and illegitimately by a white bootlegger). *Ashini*, with its Indian victim resisting alien intrusions into his culture, deals more obviously with Québec's threatened position vis à vis the "English" outside world. *Agaguk*, incidentally, has a happy ending and *Ashini* a tragic one. But the syllogistic identification is there, in this case "We as French Canadians are to the English as the natives are to the whites," that is, exploited victims threatened with extinction.

Leonard Cohen in his novel *Beautiful Losers* does with the Indian-victim motif what Graeme Gibson does with the animal-victim one: he pushes it to its most logical conclusion. *Beautiful Losers* depicts not only the sufferings of the victim, but the mentality of the Canadian onlooker who needs to identify with victims. The protagonist is a folklorist who has deliberately chosen as his subject a totally abject and failed tribe of Indians. This tribe, the A——s (they aren't even allowed a full name), epitomize the "losers" who give the book its title. The tribe has only ten members left:

> Their brief history is characterized by incessant defeat. The very name of the tribe, A——, is the word for corpse in the language of all the neighbouring tribes. There is no record that this unfortunate people ever won a single battle, while the songs and legends of its enemies are virtually nothing but a sustained howl of triumph.

"My interest in this pack of failures betrays my character," the protagonist comments on himself. "Borrowing money from me, F often said: Thanks, you old A——!"

The protagonist, in brief, is a victim who needs to be a victim, and his interest in the A—— tribe is a symptom of this need. The two women he is obsessed with are further symptoms: they are both masochists, they are both Indians and they are both dead. One is his former wife Edith, who has been raped at the age of fourteen by four white men and who later commits suicide by squashing herself under an elevator. The other is an early Canadian "saint," Catherine Tekakwitha; she was an adept at flagellation and self-mortification, and the protagonist revels in long fantasies constructed around her experiments with thorn shirts and fasting. It is their capacity for suffering he identifies with. "Is it surprising," he asks, "that I've tunnelled through libraries after news about victims?" The astute reader can only answer "No."

The written history of Catherine Tekakwitha is donated to the protagonist by his dead friend, lover, wife's lover and *alter ego*, F. F was once a partisan of the *Québec Libre* movement and has blown up a statue of the Queen of England, losing his thumb in the process. He ends his days in a hospital for the criminally insane, recalling his sexual experiments with Edith which have been abetted by (among other things) a recitation of the martyrdom of Brébeuf, and which have pushed both F and Edith to the brink of personal annihilation. Among F's many asylum ruminations is one that contains an almost perfect articulation of the Victor/Victim chain (as seen by a French rather than an English Canadian):

> The English did to us what we did to the Indians, and the Americans did to the English what the English did to us. I demanded revenge for everyone. I saw cities burning, I saw movies falling into blackness. . . . I saw the Jesuits punished. I saw the trees taking back the long-house roofs. I saw the shy deer murdering to get their dresses back. I saw the Indians punished. I saw chaos eat the gold roof of Parliament. I saw water dissolve the hoofs of drinking animals. I saw the bonfires covered with urine, and the gas stations swallowed up entire, highway after highway falling into the wild swamps.

For the chain of victors and victims to be reversed, for "revenge" to be achieved for everyone, would according to F's vision involve the collapse of all forms of human civilization and their return to the chaos of Nature, to the "wild swamps." In this vision the Indian is just one victim among many; for this is a vision of total victimization in which *everything* is a victim, even the water that is being drunk by animals. Further than this it would be hard to go.

———◇———

So far we have seen Indians used in Canadian literature for two main purposes: as instruments of Nature the Monster, torturing and killing white victims; and as variants themselves of the victim motif. Canadian writers seem to have been less interested in Indians and Eskimos *per se* than they have been in Indians and Eskimos as exotic participants in their own favourite game. Both of these uses keep the Indian closed inside Position Two, the position within which Victors and Victims are inevitable, fated to suffer and to inflict suffering because that's what the universe is like. Indian as tormentor and Indian as sufferer both permit the author the same kind of identification – identification with a victim, whether white or red – and the same necessity-bound outlook. To free the players from endless role-swapping involves a move to Position Three, where suffering is not regarded as unavoidable. This would not mean the destruction of everything, as F's vision would have it, but a rejection of the Victor/Victim game itself, as it includes Indians. It's problematical whether or not that can happen until it happens in society itself, but here at any rate are some instances that suggest there may be other literary possibilities.

In *Beautiful Losers*, as well as *Klee Wyck*, the Indians are not just victims. They are also a potential source of magic, of a knowledge about the natural-supernatural world which the white man renounced when he became "civilized." This

and it ends

> when you see the land naked, look again
> (burn your maps, that is not what I mean),
> I mean the moment when it seems most plain
> is the moment when you must begin again

Exploration seems compulsive (you *must* begin again) but it is also never-ending: you can't *find* anything or get anywhere permanent. Of course this may be interpreted as a general this-is-what-life-is-like poem, but in view of the next two poems it is also very Canadian.

The next poem is called "The Portage," and it too is about the impossibility of getting anywhere, though the images it uses are more specifically Canadian: portages and canoes, Indian drums. The explorers are explorers of self, but the image for self is an unknown land:

> We have travelled far with ourselves
> and our names have lengthened;
>   we have carried ourselves
> on our backs, like canoes
> in a strange portage, over trails. . . .
> seeking the edge, the end,
> the coastlines of this land.

But the speaker finds herself in an autumn landscape, unprepared for winter and devoid even of a sense of purpose, though undecipherable messages being sent by Indians are "trying to tell us / why we have come." Nothing has been discovered and the exploration seems to have come to at least a temporary end:

But now we fear movement
and now we dread stillness
. . . .
we are in sympathy with the fallen
trees; we cannot relate
   the causes of our grief.
We can no more carry
our boats our selves
over these insinuating trails.

The third poem. "Night on Gull Lake," has even more specific imagery based on a "realistic" canoe trip. This time the explorers, travelling by borrowed boat, have ended up on an island. They wonder whether they're the first to find and name it (no answer). Nothing much happens except that they spend a rather cold night. The poem ends,

When we took off over
the shallow waves next day
   our pockets were full
of pebbles that we knew
we'd throw away,
and when we turned around
to see the island
one last time, it was lost
in fog and it
had never quite been found.

All that has been found are some pebbles that will be discarded; all that has been discovered is the impossibility of discovering.

Douglas LePan's poem "A Country Without A Mythology" is another exploration poem of this type, except that the terrain being explored is more obviously the Canadian state of mind; again, nothing is found. For a somewhat different approach to this non-discovery kind of exploration poem, there's John Newlove's "Samuel Hearne in Wintertime," in which the poet plays with the temptation to make his version of the explorer's trip a journey into a "romantic world," but rejects this as a fantasy enjoyable for people whose "houses are heated / to some degree." Instead he postulates Sam's journey as a journey into squalor, with camps that "smelled / like hell," undertaken for practical purposes: the explorer wanted "to know, to do a job." Although Newlove insists that Sam "did more / in the land . . . . than endure," we aren't sure what more, or what he comes to "know"; perhaps it is the death at the end of the poem, the death of an Eskimo girl, which Sam, "helpless" before his "helpers," cannot prevent. This is the note on which the poem ends: the explorer as a helpless witness of death.

A short story which epitomizes this view of exploration is Matt Cohen's fantasy "Columbus and the Fat Lady." It is in fact a very Canadian version of the discovery of America, in which Columbus is hardly a triumphant discoverer of a new continent. Because he has somehow got his times mixed up and has arrived too late, he is forced to work as a sideshow freak, giving a recital each night of the horrors of the voyage and collapsing each time in a cold sweat of terror. His memories of his life in Spain are of tortures and deaths, his life in the present is haunted (understandably) by a feeling of utter placelessness; he has discovered nothing and understands nothing except that it has all somehow gone hideously wrong.

The second kind of exploration motif, the doomed exploration, is also a Canadian favourite. It is present, in tone if not explicitly, in Eli Mandel's short poem "From the North Saskatchewan":

when on the high bluff discovering
the river cuts below
                    send messages
we have spoken to those on the boats. . . .

         . . . .

I cannot read the tree markings

today the sky is torn by wind:
a field after a long battle
strewn with corpses of cloud

give blessings to my children
speak for us to those who sent us here

say we did all that could be done
we have not learned
what lies north of the river
or past those hills that look like beasts

Here the narrator has been sent by someone unknown to find out something he has been unable to discover; he's on a failed quest. His inability to read the tree markings, the cloud-as-corpse imagery, the blessings sent to the children (deathbed blessings?) and the beast-like hills all indicate not only that his mission has failed but that he won't make it back (wherever "back" is) alive.

The epitome of the doomed-exploration motif can be found in a remarkable poem for voices by Gwendolyn MacEwen called *Terror and Erebus*. It's about the Franklin expedition in search of the Northwest Passage, which of course was a disaster. MacEwen intersperses excerpts from journals with the voices of Franklin and Crozier, and of Rasmussen, who later found the Passage. The result is an eerie narrative in which what the explorers find themselves exploring, in their ordeal in the ships and later their hopeless trek across the ice, is the limits of their own human endurance and the shape of their own death. As Rasmussen, addressing Franklin, says,

> The earth insists
> There is but one geography, but then
> There is another still,
> The complex, crushed geography of men.

Looked at in the context of the "doomed exploration" motif, Duncan Campbell Scott's well-known poem "The Piper of Arll" takes on new contours. It too is a doomed exploration poem. The explorer, the Piper himself, is dead before he sets out; the ship on which he might have sailed, albeit as a corpse, becomes paralyzed, as do the sailors on it, and finally sinks. What the expedition discovers finally is the bottom of the sea, the realm of death and the unconscious; but even this discovery is a singularly static one, as the sailors and the corpse of the Piper have become a fixed *tableau* of begemmed and metallic figures.

———◁◦▷———

The exploration motifs we've been looking at have obvious relations to the victim themes explored earlier, except that in the exploration theme there is no visible victor or persecutor; possibly the core of the pattern is "failure" rather than "victim," though both are aspects of the same attitude (the victim blames someone else, the failure himself, if anyone; but both are losers).

There's another area in which you might find variations of "explorer" motifs; I'm thinking of those poems and stories in which Canadians retrace their original journey and return to Europe (or other "older" parts of the world) as tourists or expatriates. It would be interesting to compare their reactions with those of American travellers such as Henry James or Hemingway. I could make a few guesses as to what you would find, but you can probably deduce already what those would be.

———◇———

SETTLERS

In MacEwen's poem, Franklin tries to impose order on the Arctic chaos he is trapped and dying in, and fails. Usually explorers enter chaos and emerge from it; they do not try to impose order on it. That's an activity more characteristic of settlers. They do not move through the land, they go to one hitherto uncleared part of it and attempt to change Nature's order (which may look to man like chaos) into the shape of human civilization: houses, fenced plots of ground with edible plants inside and weeds outside, roads; and, later and for purposes other than survival, churches, jails, schools, hospitals and graveyards. The order of Nature is labyrinthine, complex, curved; the order of Western European Man tends to squares, straight lines, oblongs and similar shapes. (The basic Canadian town is laid out like a checkerboard, perhaps on the model of the garrisons from which such towns often sprang.) So the Canadian pioneer is a square man in a round whole; he faces the problem of trying to fit a straight line into a curved space. Of course, the *necessity* for the straight lines is not in Nature but in his own head; he might have had a happier time if he'd tried to fit himself into Nature, not the other way round.

The pattern for American "pioneers" – Pilgrim Fathers, who were definitely square men, aside – is found in Fenimore Cooper's novels. There, Natty Bumppo or Hawkeye *precedes* the settlers into the wilderness. He isn't interested in building a house or cultivating a farm; he lives by the natural and Indian ways of the land (corny though those ways may appear in the ornamental mirror of Cooper's prose). He moves further and further West as settlement follows in his wake, bringing with it law and order; he is moving to *escape* law and order, and when he and his literary descendants get far enough West they turn into the Wild West. The only thing like him in Canadian history are probably the *coureurs de bois* and early French explorers; Canada never had a Wild West, for the simple reason that the Mounties got there first. Law and Order and the garrison with its palisade were there before the Natty Bumppos and the settlers hit town.

There's an awful American movie called *How the West Was Won* that takes the bored and writhing viewer across America by prairie schooner, through a few brawls and Indian fights and young girls saying "But Maw . . ." and ends with a shot of the Los Angeles freeway, clogged with traffic, that is supposed to be triumphant (in Canada it would be ironic, and when I saw it here there were a lot of boos and mocking cheers). But however vile the movie, the sentiments it embodies are (as they say) American as apple pie: the West was something to be conquered and claimed. The West, or the wilderness, is in Canadian fiction much more likely to come through as a place of exile: there are the settlers, come from the old country with their European artefacts, building their walls within which they hope to recreate that old country; they don't have to *really* fight because the Mounties are there, the rules of the game are set up already, the flag is flying. No outlaws or lawless men for Canada; if one appears, the Mounties always get their man.

This is not necessarily a bad thing, but it *is* a very different thing. It both reflects and reinforces a view of the universe based not on the eighteenth-century American version of "freedom" in which man is supposedly free to shape his own destiny (and if that destiny is manifest and involves conquest, what can withstand it?) but on a vision of order as inherent in the universe. This in fact must have been a much more difficult vision to sustain in the face of the North American continent. And it does indicate why the first presence of the Mounties and the absence of a Wild West are neither omissions nor accidents: law is there first because the universe is conceived as being already under its sway. The presence or absence of law is not thought of as something determined more or less arbitrarily by a shoot-em-out or display of strength at High Noon. This Canadian attitude towards law can work positively or negatively, and there will always be men and governments around who will claim that they are the sole embodiments of the Universal Order; but the presence of the attitude is undeniable. (George Grant explores it in his two books, *Lament for a Nation* and *Technology and Empire*.)

What interests us about it is the problem it raises in connection with the Settler theme: Canadian settler figures are less likely to see their activities as the construction of a new world built according to their free fancies than the implementation of an order that is "right." The imposition of the straight line on the curve tends to get seen by those doing the imposing as part of the Divine Plan, and that can lead to a good deal of intolerance and rigidity; the American way, by contrast, can lead to a good deal of violence.

The Settler theme in Canadian literature breaks down – and again this is a guess – into two motifs:

- Straight line battles curve and wins, but destroys human "life force" in the process.
- Straight line deteriorates and curve takes over again; that is, settlement fails.

Because of the relatively late emergence of fiction in Canada, most of our good early-settler *fiction* deals with the prairies; whereas the elegiac reflections and meditations on relics of a vanished past in *poetry* tend to come more often from Ontario or the Maritimes. The first motif spawns a good many will-driven patriarchs, and one of the best places to look for them is in the novels of Frederick Philip Grove. There's Ellen's father in *Settlers of the Marsh*, clearing the land and building his farm, praying fervently at night and proclaiming that God has been good to him while at the same time driving his wife into the ground by a combination of hard work, forced impregnation and equally forced miscarriages. The father is imposing his pattern of straight lines – barn, house, fence – on the curved land, and the wife and her fertility are a part of the "curved" Nature he is trying to control. But instead of controlling her he kills her, both spiritually (she comes to hate him) and physically. He kills also the ability to love in his daughter Ellen. The blockage of life-energy that results when Ellen refuses to marry the protagonist finally precipitates a murder. There are the Clarks in *The Master of the Mill*, in which the straight-line edifice is the mill and the curve upon which it's imposed is the rest of life. There's John Elliott in *Our Daily Bread* and Abe Spaulding in *The Fruits of the Earth*. In all these cases the settlers succeed in their plan, build their straight-line constructions, but kill something vital in the process; it is often Nature in the form of a woman. The pattern can be caught at its starting-point in a story by another Western writer, "Carrion Spring" by Wallace Stegner. Again, the man is going to impose his will on the land; and again, it's a woman who will be ground down in the process. At the moment when she agrees to stay and help her husband set up a ranch, the heroine is "sick and scared," and no wonder.

When you set this motif – straight line wins over curve – against its opposite, the total picture is one of futility. That is, straight line defeats curve and kills vital energy by doing so; but then the straight-line edifice itself crumbles, and nothing has been accomplished except a lot of wasted suffering. The poems Canadians tend to make out of "settler" motifs are likely to end, not with a shot of the Los Angeles freeway or equivalent, but with the abandonment of the farm with its squares and angles and the takeover of Nature once again. The pattern is struggle without result. The quotation from Dennis Lee at the beginning of the chapter, with its broken settlers and "brute surroundings," illustrates this very well. So does an excellent poem by Al Purdy, called "The Country North of Belleville," in which the wilderness has been settled and then largely abandoned, and the landscape is strewn with deserted farms:

> And where the farms have gone back
> to forest
>
> > are only soft outlines and
> > shadowy differences –
>
> Old fences drift vaguely among the trees
> > a pile of moss-covered stones
> gathered for some ghost purpose

has lost meaning under the meaningless sky
  – they are like cities under water and
the undulating green waves of time
  are laid on them. . . .

"This is a country where the young leave quickly," Purdy says; and though he concludes with the possibility of a return to "the country of our defeat," where "the high townships of Cashel / McClure and Marmora once were," he admits he no longer remembers how to get there:

  . . . it's been a long time since
  and we must enquire the way
  of strangers –

You could make a whole anthology of Canadian poems about tumbled-down houses and deserted farms. But I'll end with a brief mention of two of my own experimental constructions of ancestral totems from this kind of material. The first is the poem "Progressive Insanities of a Pioneer," in which the settler makes a division between himself with his straight-line house and fence and the Nature on which he is trying to impose his own ideas of order. He fails, and in the end his head is invaded by the Nature which he has identified as chaos, refusing to recognize that it has its own kind of order. He is insane by the end of the poem; but, as the title implies, perhaps he was insane at its beginning: the attempts to impose this kind of order by a suppression of everything "curved" may itself be a form of madness. (From the point of view of Nature, a house is an act of arrogance. . . .)

The second is the book *The Journals of Susanna Moodie*, which explores more fully the tensions between straight line and curve. I tend to be on the side of the curve, and I haven't yet decided whether that stance is Position Two defeatism (don't build a fence because it will fall down anyway) or Position Four acceptance of life-as-process (don't build a fence because you'll be keeping out things you should be letting in).

———◇———

These, then, are the prevailing shapes which (I speculate) our writers have given to two of the mythic ancestral figures on the collective totem pole: Explorers who fail or die, Settlers whose suffering and effort is futile. Some redemption might be possible if they at least enjoyed the process of travelling or building; but on the whole they're fairly grim-lipped about it.

Which leads us into the Family Portrait.

Short List:

GROVE, F. P., *Settlers of the Marsh*; NCL, $1.95.

Long List:

ATWOOD, Margaret, *The Journals of Susanna Moodie*; OUP.

ATWOOD, Margaret, "Progressive Insanities of a Pioneer," *The Animals in That Country*; OUP. Also G&B.

BIRNEY, Earle, "David," *The Poems of Earle Birney*; NCL.

COHEN, Matt, *Columbus and the Fat Lady*; AN.

GRANT, George, *Lament for a Nation*; M&S.

GRANT, George, *Technology and Empire*; AN.

GROVE, Frederick Philip, *Fruits of the Earth*; NCL.

GROVE, Frederick Philip, *The Master of the Mill*; NCL.

GROVE, Frederick Philip, *Our Daily Bread*; OP.

GROVE, Frederick Philip, *Settlers of the Marsh*; NCL.

GROVE, Frederick Philip, "Snow," WI.

KLEIN, A. M., "Portrait of the Poet as Landscape," *The Rocking Chair*; R. Also *Poets Between the Wars* (ed. Milton Wilson); NCL.

LePAN, Douglas, "A Country Without a Mythology," *The Book of Canadian Poetry* (ed. A. J. M. Smith); Gage.

MacEWEN, Gwen, "The Discovery," *The Shadow Maker*; Macmillan. Also in G&B.

MacEWEN, Gwen, *Terror and Erebus*; CBC (not in print).

MANDEL, Eli, "From the North Saskatchewan," G&B.

NEWLOVE, John, "Samuel Hearne in Wintertime," *Black Night Window*; M&S. Also ML.

PURDY, Al, "The Country North of Belleville," M. Also *Selected Poems*; M&S.

PURDY, Al, "Private Property," *Wild Grape Wine*; M&S.

PRATT, E. J., "The Titanic," *Selected Poems*; Macmillan.

SCOTT, Duncan Campbell, "The Piper of Arll," *Poets of the Confederation* (ed. Malcolm Ross); NCL.

SCOTT, Frederick George, "The Unnamed Lake," *The Book of Canadian Poetry* (ed. A. J. M. Smith); Gage.

STEGNER, Wallace, "Carrion Spring," *Stories from Western Canada* (ed. Wiebe); Macmillan.

6

FAMILY PORTRAIT:

MASKS OF THE BEAR

In the great echoing vault of history
Our names are not heard.
Less than conquerors, we were not at Marathon,
And if we died in battle it was the mud
And not the battle we were most aware of. . . .
. . . .
Sons, daughters (soon to be brothers and sisters
When death makes us all contemporary)
Do not forget us because we were not great men.
It is we, more than saints, soldiers or poets
Who have broken the soil for you,
Built houses and languages for you.

– Elizabeth Brewster,
"Local Graveyard"

My grandparents lived to a great age in the cold –
O cruel preservative, the hard day beginning
With night and zero and the firewood
Numbing the fingers.
. . . .
                    . . . They lived in cold
And were seasoned by it and preached it
And knew that it blazed
In the burning bush of antiquity
With starry flowers.

– Dorothy Roberts,
"Cold"

Mackenzie had told him that although he might be an intellectual agnostic, he was an emotional child in thrall to his barbarous Presbyterian past. As he thought this, he felt guilty again. But why? Was there no end to the circle of Original Sin? Could a man never grow up and be free?

– *Hugh MacLennan,*
Each Man's Son

In some families, *please* is described as the magic word. In our house, however, it was *sorry.*

– *Margaret Laurence,*
A Bird in the House

Strung out one by one, we move together
through the landscape. Children and parents.

– *Tom Wayman,*
"Opening the Family"

This chapter looks at what our writers have made of the society which came into being after exploration and settlement. Since this society is most often examined in our literature through the three-generational or Family Portrait novel, the chapter is in fact a study of the literary family. Canada has no monopoly on families, and Grandfathers, Parents and Children can be found anywhere; however, it's the traits assigned by Canadian writers to these three generations that are of interest.

There are several ways in which the Canadian approach to the family is distinct from the English and American approaches, and this takes us back to our three core symbols, the English Island, the American Frontier, and the Canadian Survival. In English literature the family – the extended family, composed of distant ancestors and relatives of all kinds, cousins reckoned up by dozens, numberless aunts – is a structure *within* which, and in terms of which, the characters grow and develop. (Think of *The Forsyte Saga*.) The hero seldom really breaks away: even if he has a tiff with his family he still views himself, and is viewed by them, as a member. It's like the Catholic Church, you can't really leave it. Wherever you move on the Island, you are still on the Island.

In American literature the family is something the hero must repudiate and leave; it is the structure he rebels against, thereby defining his own freedom, his own Frontier. *You Can't Go Home Again*, as the Thomas Wolfe novel has it. Once out you're out, you must forge your own life, your own private America, out of whatever new materials you can find. An American "family" scene that's repeated over and over is the hero at the train station, lighting out for the Territory. Sons must *by definition* transcend their fathers, in the process rejecting them. The family, then, is something you come from and get rid of (unless you're from the South; then you commit suicide because you *can't* get rid of it).

In Canadian literature the family is handled quite differently. If in England the family is a mansion you live in, and if in America it's a skin you shed, then in Canada it's a trap in which you're caught. The Canadian protagonist often feels just as trapped inside his family as his American counterpart; he feels the need for escape, but somehow he is unable to break away. Two examples that come to mind immediately are David Cannan, trapped on the farm and longing for the outside world in Buckler's *The Mountain and the Valley*, and the boy in Raymond Knister's story "Mist Green Oats," also trapped on the farm and longing for the outside world. But the Canadian protagonist's sense of entrapment is likely to be balanced by an equally strong sense of preservation: not self-preservation, but group preservation, Survival again. Families in Canadian fiction huddle together like sheep in a storm or chickens in a coop: miserable and crowded, but unwilling to leave because the alternative is seen as cold empty space. I'd say that this pattern is as true, if not truer, in the literature of French Canada as it is in that of English Canada, though it is more likely there to be symbolized by blocked incestuous love.

The ingrown-toenail family-as-trap, often presided over by a rigid domineering Grandfather (or a rigid domineering Grandmother, though the suppressive element is more likely to be male) can create a reasonably unpleasant situation. At its most unpleasant it is mirrored in the Decaying-heritage motif, in which the family and the structures that have maintained it are rotting away, generating in the process a lurid gothic light. See for instance Eli Mandel's poem "Estevan, Saskatchewan," which begins "A small town bears the mark of Cain" and proceeds to develop this theme with references to warped family relationships, blighted harvests and mad children.

The heritage as booby-trap is a milder version of this; you can see it in operation in two stories, "The Heritage" by Ringuet and "The Legacy" by Mavis Gallant. In Ringuet's story the hitherto rootless protagonist inherits a tobacco farm from a dead father who has not acknowledged him during his lifetime. He moves onto the farm and work, but for some reason it stops raining, the tobacco plants dry up, and he leaves again, having gained nothing but another experience of failure and a rather strange girl-friend, a loser like himself. Mavis Gallant's story is more complex. Four grown up children have met after their mother's funeral in the slum store where they grew up. Two of the sons are habitual criminals; the third has "made good," got an education, moved to the States and married an American wife, who announces with pride that they own their own home. The fourth child is a spinster schoolteacher who now teaches at the same school she herself attended. The mother has left the store to the "good" son, who renounces it after the other three accuse him of having been the cause of the sister's blighted life: the money that was to have taken her to France on a scholarship was used by the mother to pay off two policemen who caught him committing his one and only criminal offence. What comes through most strongly in the story is the sister's sense of entrapment by her family: the "good" brother has followed the American plan of repudiation, but she has followed the Canadian plan, from which she derives no satisfaction. As the "good" brother puts it, "She blames me because I got out and she never had the guts." The final ignominy comes when the two remaining brothers try to foist the store on her as a compensation gift:

. . . Marina flung out her arm, almost striking him as she threw the key away. 'For me?' she cried again. 'I'm to live here?' She looked around as if to find, once more, the path away from St. Eulalie Street, the shifting and treacherous path that described a circle, and if her brothers, after the first movement, had not held her fast, she would have wrecked the room. . . .

The joke is that Marina is fighting off entrapment, but in fact she's already been trapped. "The shifting and treacherous path that described a circle" is a good summation of the route taken by Canadian fictional characters in their unsuccessful efforts to escape from their families.

Both of these legacy stories involve only two generations; however, the complete pattern is composed of three: Grandparents, Parents, and third-generation Children. A lot of what is said about three-generation novels here can also be applied to another variety of the *genre*, the "Immigrant" novels treated separately in Chapter Seven; the ones we are talking about here usually concern families of Scots Presbyterian descent, though the ethic in other groups is often not all that different. It's worth mentioning too that the Grandfather, Parent and Child *roles* in fiction are not always the same as the actual generations, though they are likely to be; that is, the son of a Grandfather, instead of attempting a second-generation escape, may simply choose to play a Grandfather role himself.

Here then is a rough outline, as extracted from numerous novels, of the characteristics of the three roles.

Grandparents are not necessarily Settlers, though because of the nature of Canadian history it's possible for the two to be the same. Canadian history is very short; it is also – due to the rapidity with which settlement was followed by industrialization – very squashed together. The explorers for us are semi-mythic figures like King Arthur and the settlers are like the late middle ages, with British and French forts and square-timbered log shacks the closest thing we have to castles. But in fact none of that happened very long ago. It is even possible for people from the West to remember grandparents who were settlers. The nineteenth century, which in England is practically modern times, is for us the remote past, partly because of the greater difference in styles of living between then and now. So though grandparents may in some cases be equivalent with settlers, by "grandfathers" I really mean those who took over from the settlers, inherited whatever had been built.

As well as inheriting the physical structures and the assumptions of the society constructed by the Settlers, the Grandfathers are usually seen as inheriting also the character traits necessary for the attempted imposition of a rigid order on the land. But instead of pitting their force of will against the land – that's been done for them by *their* ancestors – they pit it against other people, most notably their descendants. Grandparents may be treated as isolated subjects in poems, and such poems emphasize most often their negative strengths, the fervour with which they disapprove and repress; but in fiction the Grandfather is related to the two other generations, each acting out a variant of the family curse. Grandparents are obsessed by work; they have unbending wills and sets of "principles," which the author may feel his own generation has lost. They are grimly religious, and more than willing to police and censor the morals of others. They rule, or attempt to rule, their children with a rod of iron. They are patriarchs and matriarchs, and their cosmic rigidity goes far beyond the strength necessary to build and sustain a pioneering community.

The grandfather as rigid and threatening icon, self-proclaimed embodiment of morality and the Calvinist Will of God, is glimpsed in full flower in George Bowering's poem "Grandfather." Suitably enough, this Grandfather is a preacher:

> Grandfather
> Jabez Harry Bowering
> strode across the Canadian prairie
> hacking down trees
> and building churches
> delivering personal baptist sermons in them
> leading Holy holy holy lord god almighty songs
> in them. . . .

He comes from England to "apocalyptic Canada," makes it through Ontario "of bone bending child labour," and arrives in Brandon, Manitoba, where he

> . . . built his first wooden church and married
> a sick girl who bore two live children and died
> leaving several pitiful letters and the Manitoba night . . .

He gets another wife and moves further west, until finally "lord god almighty"

> . . . struck his labored bones with pain
> and left him a postmaster prodding grandchildren
> with crutches
> another dead wife and a glass bowl of photographs
> and holy books unopened save the bible by the bed

> Till he died the day before his eighty fifth birthday
> in a Catholic hospital of sheets white as his hair

The tree-hacking, the sermons, the two dead wives, and the grandfather's end – especially the prodding of grandchildren with crutches – are exemplary for Canadian grandfathers.

Parents (the middle generation) try to escape. They may move from a farm to a town, from a town to a big city. But they have internalized the guilt foisted on them by the Grandparents, and they do not often make a great success of their lives. They lack the will, the attachment to the land and the metallic strength of their parents, but they have been unable to replace it with any-thing more positive and attractive. They are somehow crippled; or they are vague, lacking in definition; or they are just as work-driven as the Grandparents but without the compensation of being able to believe that they are fulfilling the Will of God.

Children try to escape both previous generations. They desire neither the Calvinism and commitment to the land of the Grandparents, nor the grey placelessness and undefined guilt of the Parents. They want, somehow, to *live*, but they have trouble finding a way to do this. They sometimes feel a double pull – back to the tough values and the land, like the Grandparents, or away – farther away than the Parents managed to get – to Europe, an escape they may identify with personal and sexual liberation (and if, as so often happens, they have ambitions as artists, with Art). But if they do manage the great escape, they most typically join groups of mediocre artists; if they are artists themselves, they usually fail at it. (See Chapter Nine for more failed artists.)

The three generations are not always present in this clear a pattern in every "generational" novel, but you can find them wandering about, alone or in pairs, in much Canadian fiction. Grandparents and Parents are there in Ringuet's *Thirty Acres*, with its old man whom the land has failed and the son who has become urbanized. Grandparents alone dominate Hémon's

Maria Chapdelaine, since Maria refuses the chance to move off the land to the city and become a middle-generation Parent, choosing instead to remain on the land and become her own mother, a Grandparent.

Margaret Laurence's *The Stone Angel* has some model Grandparents. Hagar Shipley's stern father is a perfect Grandfather figure, and Hagar tries to rebel against him by marrying a source of earth energy, the disreputable but attractive farmer Bram. But she has soaked up too many of her father's principles, and she stifles Bram with her disapproval of him; instead of achieving liberation she has turned into a Grandparent herself. Of her two sons, one takes the path of Parents and goes to the city, where he turns brownish-grey. The other tries to be a Child, in search of liberation, but there's not much scope for him; and when Hagar discovers his love affair and tortures him with her disapproval and moral rigidity, he gets himself killed in an accident.

In the fiction of Morley Callaghan and Hugh Garner, in the poems of Raymond Souster, characters from the Parent generation abound – losers and marginal men of the town or city. They are there too in the novels of Hugh MacLennan, with their guilt-ridden protagonists who somehow can't manage to live fully. Pathos is the basic mode, and a very qualified success is all anyone can ever hope to achieve. Hugh Garner's *The Silence on the Shore*, with its Toronto Annex rooming house filled with cramped souls, is a good place to Parent-hunt. "Don't fight life until it's too late to live it," an alcoholic says, from bitter experience, to an overly-religious young girl. "Live it now." That is the message the Parents have for the Children; that, plus the ever-present rhetorical Canadian question, voiced through another Garner loser: "Do any of us ever win?"

Focus is on the Parent generation in Hugh MacLennan's

novel *Each Man's Son*. The main protagonist is Dr. Ainslie, a compulsive worker riddled with a guilt instilled in him by his Calvinist father, a Grandfather if ever there was one:

> The face of his father flashed before his eyes. How could he ever hope to win the kind of struggle such a father had bred into his son? The old Calvinist had preached that life was a constant struggle against evil, and his son had believed him. At the same time he had preached that failure was a sin. Now the man who had been the boy must ask, How could a successful man be sinless, or a sinless man successful?

Ainslie's thoughts go round and round like this even though he technically no longer believes in "God." The father, like Grove's patriarchs, has been a wife-killer (he deprived his family of food so he could use the money to build an ambition-satisfying barn); Dr. Ainslie himself manages a version of this when he accidentally, but symbolically, sterilizes his own wife during an operation. The Child generation is present in the young boy Alan, chosen by Ainslie as his surrogate son, upon whom Ainslie tries to inflict his values in a way that recalls his own father's similar behaviour. At the end of the book Alan's real father – a punch-drunk prize-fighter ruined in the States – returns and kills both the boy's mother and her suitor, leaving Alan to be brought up by the Ainslies. Ainslie gets his "son," but it's a dubious victory, bought at the price of blood, and it's clear the child, having been witness to the double murder, will be warped in some essential way. The book is set against a background of permanent losers – Cape Breton miners – and in at least ten important places MacLennan uses images of wounded or frightened animals to describe his gallery of the spiritually maimed. (MacLennan's novel is a good demonstration of how a number of the themes we've been investigating dove-tail into one another.)

The generation of the Children can be found in the fiction of Alice Munro and Marian Engel. Munro's brilliant story "The Peace of Utrecht" has all three generations: Grandparents in the rather mild form of two old great-aunts, Parents in the form of a grotesque mother crippled with a wasting disease which has made it difficult for her to speak, and Children in the form of two daughters. One, the narrator, has escaped into marriage; the other, Maddy, has been trapped in the small town with the sick mother. Finding herself unable to live her own life, she puts the mother in a hospital where she quickly dies, leaving Maddy burdened with nothing more than the disapproval of the aunts. But somehow she *still* can't live. "I couldn't go on," she says, "I wanted my life." Her sister urges her to leave:

> "Take your life, Maddy. Take it."
> "Yes I will,' Maddy said. 'Yes I will."
> "Go away, don't stay here."
> "Yes I will."

However, the last words of the story are spoken by Maddy: "But why can't I, Helen? *Why can't I?*"

Marian Engel's novel *The Honeyman Festival* explores some of the reasons why she can't. Minn, the heroine, has already made her escape from the generational trap: she's been to Europe, where she's had an affair with a second-rate film director. But the novel picks her up at the point where she is back in Canada, pregnant and trapped, both physically in her own body and in a crumbling Toronto-Victorian house and spiritually in her memories, especially those of the preceding generations. Her

Grandparent generation is represented by her mother Gertrude, a corseted, rigid, strong-willed matron who forces her to scrub toilets; her Parent generation by her father, a greyish, spineless man nicknamed Weeping Willie. Minn's stab at personal and sexual liberation has left her still partly in bondage; now she must attempt to come to terms with her hometown of Godwin (what a Protestant Ethic name!) and with the internalized demands and taboos of her ancestors. You can't just leave it all behind, as the narrator realizes also in "The Peace of Utrecht": Minn discovers that a certain amount of exorcism, acceptance and reconciliation is needed, though there's no sure sign that she achieves them sufficiently for her other life-energies to be freed.

Guilt, guilt and more guilt. But for the Children, even more than for the Parents, it is a guilt without final cause and therefore a guilt without final atonement or expiation. The further into the past the Calvinist God recedes, the more his legacy of guilt becomes separated from its objects: Children can feel guilty about *everything*. Books such as Russell Marois' *The Telephone Pole* suggest that, for literary purposes at least, the so-called relaxation of Puritan taboos could produce, not a race of guilt-free Canadians, but simply a wider field for the exercise of guilt. For Marois' Children, guilt is something they inherit along with their genes and chromosomes; they may not even explicitly feel it, but it's like the air they breathe, and their self-destructive and nihilistic behaviour is merely an acting out of it.

———◇———

In Margaret Laurence's collection of stories, *A Bird in the House*, the three-generation pattern is displayed in virtually its pure form. The point of view is that of the child Vanessa, who wants to be a writer; she fills scribblers with romantic melodramas while at the same time eavesdropping on the real lives of the other two generations which surround her. The patriarch and matriarch of her world are her mother's father and her father's mother, who seldom meet. "If they had ever really clashed," she says, "it would have been like a brontosaurus running head-long into a tyrannosaurus." It is her Grandmother's contention that "God loves Order," and her immaculate house, ladylike pretensions and inhuman self-control are the manifestations of this belief. The Grandfather is far surlier. His habitual expression is anger; all other emotions he subjugates as ruthlessly as he subjugates those around him, criticizing all possible aspects of their lives, from their lack of promptness at meals to their friends, morals and ability to make money. Only once does the child Vanessa see her Grandfather express grief; it is after the death of his wife, and the spectacle of her Grandfather crying is more disturbing to her than the death itself. The metaphor she chooses for the old man is, with its suggestion of a shell conceal-ing a life that has been repressed to the point of extinction, a perfect one for the whole tribe of Canadian Grandfathers:

Many years later . . . I saw one day in a museum the Bear Mask of the Haida Indians. It was a weird mask. The fea-tures were ugly and yet powerful. The mouth was turned down in an expression of sullen rage. The eyes were empty caverns, revealing nothing. Yet as I looked, they seemed to draw my own eyes towards them, until I imagined I could see somewhere within that darkness a look which I knew, a lurking bewilderment. I remembered then that in the days before it became a museum piece, the mask had concealed a man.

Here the representatives of the Parent generation do not make their getaway; they remain in the small town, their lives dominated by the personalities of Grandfather and Grandmother. Both of them die young. The child Vanessa manages to escape to University, but predictably, at the moment of her departure, she says, ". . . and yet in some way which I could not define or understand, I did not feel nearly as free as I had expected to feel." We hear no word of her earlier ambitions as a writer. She returns much later to the town, and briefly revisits her Grandfather's house, the foursquare brick structure, first of its kind in the town, which he built when he was a self-styled "pioneer." It has been his garrison and is now his monument. The insight she has at this moment is that she hasn't travelled as far away as she had thought: "I had feared and fought the old man, yet he proclaimed himself in my veins."

—◁◦▷—

I've emphasized the negative qualities of the three generations at the expense of their positive ones. The positive ones are there, though they are often overshadowed. The main one is Survival. Laurence's family *does* manage to make it through the Depression whereas other families in the town don't; Garner's characters *do* manage to hang on, despite the bleakness of the lives they are trapped in; Engel's heroine endures, and even fights back a little (she bites a policeman). The ability to survive and endure is the other side of that rigid, iron-willed coin. And everybody gets a lot of work done: MacLennan's and Laurence's doctors slave away till all hours, Vanessa's mother is a compulsive house-cleaner, and so forth. And the members of the families are intensely loyal to the family: that's the positive side of entrapment. For instance, Munro's Maddy *does* stay to look after her mother, and Laurence's Aunt Edna won't tolerate criticism of the awful Grandfather from anyone outside the family.

The really positive virtue is the insistence in these books on facing the facts, grim though they may be. Romanticism and idealism are usually slapped down fairly hard, by authors as well as characters, when they manifest themselves, either in the too-young or in older people who are driven by abstract demons. Charity and loving-kindness, however, are cherished when they appear, partly because they appear so rarely. What one misses, though, is joy. After a few of these books you start wanting someone, sometime, to find something worth celebrating. Or at least to have fun.

————◦————

Having fun with Grandfather the Bear-mask and Grandmother the corseted brontosaurus, with guilty Father and trapped Mother, may seem either too frivolous or too great an expectation. But that it can be done is demonstrated by James Reaney in his Family Portrait play, *Colours in the Dark*. In his Author's Note, Reaney calls his play a "play box," and comments, "Life could be an endless procession of stories, an endless coloured comic strip, things to listen to and look at, a bottomless play box." In the play-box context, the generational figures we've been examining become toys, and the author – or the fantasizing little boy who is probably his stand-in in the play itself – plays with them by putting them through a series of pranks and charades. Though some of the guises they assume are no less frightening than those we've been observing in "realistic" fiction – Hitler, Antichrist and Lady Death are among them – the fear evoked is put to constructive use: it's raised and dissipated, and in the process the entire history and mythology of the race, the country and the family gets acted out, the purpose being to get the young child "born," to present him with his identity. As in most Reaney plays, the extremely universal and the extremely local – Jehovah and the Orange Day Parade in Stratford, cosmology and Winnipeg street names – are juxtaposed, producing in this case an incredible assemblage of objects and ideas.

The play ends with a recitation of ancestors stretching back ten generations and including all the people who would be in such a family tree if you were to draw it:

1024 great great great great great great great great-grandparents

512 great great great great great great great grandparents

256 great great great great great great grandparents

128 great great great great great grandparents

64 great great great great grandparents

32 great great great grandparents

16 great great grandparents

8 great grandparents

4 grandparents

2 parents

One child.

Reaney's generational totem pole accomplishes its purpose: it provides unity with the past, and through that unity the child's identity both as a human being and as an inhabitant of a particular place.

Though one suspects that the relative optimism of Reaney's vision – and of that in other "growing up" novels such as W. O. Mitchell's *Who Has Seen The Wind* – is possible only because the "child" point of view stops short this side of adulthood, it's still a relief that light-hearted amusement of any kind can be squeezed from the three Canadian generations.

———◁◇▷———

In terms of the Victim Positions, Canadian literary Grandparents are sometimes found in Position One, like Laurence's Grandmother in *A Bird in the House*, who always wanted to believe she was a "lady" and can't face up to the fact that the family is now poor. More often they are in Position Two, feeling oppressed by a harsh universe and a harsher Calvinist God, fighting for bare survival, and responding to their situation by becoming an incarnation, for their children, of the rigid universe they believe in. The Parent generation is usually in Position Two also, but as victims wounded by the Grandparents; they know there's something wrong with their world or with themselves, but they can't seem to change it. Children often make it as far as Position Three: they become angry, rebel and demand a more abundant life for themselves, though they may not always get it.

Hagar in *The Stone Angel* has a repertoire of positions. Her marriage to a farmer her father disapproves of is a Position Three act of rebellion, a repudiation of her father's Position Two principles; but she can't sustain her rebellion or move beyond it, and she slides back into Position Two. Her anger returns at the end of her life, and this time she is aiming for Position Four, for a state in which acts which are "truly free" will be possible. She does manage two free acts, and their seeming insignificance disappears when they are measured against the enormous weight of the imprisoning traditions she is struggling against:

I lie here and try to recall something truly free that I've done in ninety years. I can think of only two acts that might be so, both recent. One was a joke – yet a joke only as all victories are, the paraphernalia being unequal to the event's reach. The other was a lie – yet not a lie, for it was spoken at least and at last with what may perhaps be a kind of love.

Short List:

LAURENCE, Margaret, *A Bird in the House*; Popular Library, $0.95.

LAURENCE, Margaret, *The Stone Angel*; NCL, $2.50.

MacLENNAN, Hugh, *Each Man's Son*; Macmillan, Laurentian Library, $1.95.

REANEY, James, *Colours in the Dark*; Talonbooks, $2.50.

Long List:

BOWERING, George, "Grandfather," G&B.

BUCKLER, Ernest, *The Mountain and the Valley*; NCL.

ENGEL, Marian, *The Honeyman Festival*; AN.

GALLANT, Mavis, "The Legacy," W1.

GARNER, Hugh, *The Silence on the Shore*; M&S; Pocketbooks.

HÉMON, Louis, *Maria Chapdelaine*; Macmillan.

KNISTER, Raymond, "Mist Green Oats," W1.

LAURENCE, Margaret, *A Bird in the House*; Popular Library.

LAURENCE, Margaret, *The Stone Angel*; NCL.

MacLENNAN, Hugh, *Each Man's Son*; Macmillan, Laurentian Library.

MANDEL, Eli, "Estevan, Saskatchewan," *The Blasted Pine* (ed. F. R. Scott and A. J. M. Smith); Macmillan.

MAROIS, Russell, *The Telephone Pole*; AN.

MITCHELL, W. O., *Who Has Seen the Wind*; Macmillan.

MUNRO, Alice, "The Peace of Utrecht," *Dance of the Happy Shades*;
R. Also W2.
REANEY, James, *Colours in the Dark*; Talonbooks.
RINGUET, *Thirty Acres*; NCL.

7

FAILED SACRIFICES
The Reluctant Immigrant

It is meaningless to call anyone a foreigner in this country.
We are all foreigners here.

> – *John Marlyn,*
> Under the Ribs of Death

———————

I speak a language I have never learned,
I do not belong to any nation,
I hurl sharp poems at the world
And keep looking at the wounds in my skin
At their point of penetration.

> – *George Jonas,*
> "Five More Lines"

———————

Looking into their eyes you could see
tremendous kinds of hope:
Studebaker or Buick,
refrigerator, radio, a house,
and enough to eat always.
Some of the young men walked
with a sway of the hip
as if they had conquered Montreal (which none
                                    of them knew)
or all the gold-mines of the north.
And like a messianic pronouncement
one word was heard again and again:
money.

> – *Walter Bauer,*
> "Emigrants"

———————

He's wanted to go back
since that first spring:
1920 and the frost
rending the crops
with its cold and passionate
Canadian hands.

There's never been enough.
The army worms ate up
the first fare home,
floods took the second. . . .

– *Alden Nowlan,*
"Alex Duncan"

One of the first full-length prose works by an English-speaking immigrant to Canada – Moodie's *Roughing It in The Bush* – was written for the express purpose of telling others *not* to come, and that purpose seems to have set a precedent. Although Moodie passed en route through several already established cities, her destination was a bush farm, and it is her encounters with the land, not her encounters with urban society, that form the subject of her book. But there is a large and rapidly-growing body of literature which deals with the experiences of later immigrants, twentieth-century ones, who arrived when the time for bush-farming and settling the prairies had passed. The characters in these novels and stories make their way to cities and find themselves confronted not by uncleared land which they must transform but by patterns of urban society which they seem to have no hope of transforming.

Are their experiences with the city more promising or fulfilling than earlier immigrants' experiences with the land? Certainly they are similarly disturbing. Both earlier and later immigrants come unprepared and are confused by what they find; but for the later immigrants, hostile cities replace hostile forests, and the place of the feared, unfriendly and treacherous natives has been taken by – of course – those earlier immigrants, the WASPS and the French.

American literature also has examples of what we may call the Immigrant Novel; though the ratio is lower, due to the U.S. shutdown on immigration *circa* 1900 and the ideological pressure to assimilate. In both Canadian and American immigrant novels, there is usually a tension between the cultural values of the "old" society and that of the new one, with members of the first generation often electing to stick with the old values and members of the second wishing to abandon them in favour of the new; and, sometimes, members of the third generation functioning as symbols of integration.

The difference is in the outcome. In a typical American plot, the immigrant throws away his old values (usually hierarchical and paternalistic) and espouses egalitarian democracy. The price America demands is a leap into the melting pot: he must attempt – and often he desires – to efface all traces of his ethnic origins in order to become a real "American," to take on a new identity. His reward is material success, sanctioned by American ideology. At this point the plot may take an ironic turn: he sacrifices his ancestral identity to become successful and finds success hollow. A typical Canadian plot has certain important differences. First, Canada does not demand a leap into the melting pot, though the immigrant may decide to attempt one anyway. Secondly, if he does wipe away his ethnic origin, there is no new "Canadian" identity ready for him to step into: he is confronted only by a nebulosity, a blank; no ready-made ideology is provided for him. And thirdly, though he has sacrificed his past and tried for success, he is much more likely to find only failure. The sacrifice has been made for nothing: not nothing plus money, just nothing. Some Canadian novels follow the American pattern – one thinks of Mordecai Richler's *The Apprenticeship of Duddy Kravitz*, with its ghetto hero who climbs to fortune over the bodies of relatives and friends (though Duddy's symbol of success is Canadian – a piece of land, not a block of stocks), and who reappears, rich but de-energized, in a later Richler novel, *St. Urbain's Horseman*. But for most writers failure in Canada has evidently been easier to imagine than success.

Morley Callaghan's story, "Last Spring They Came Over," is especially useful in a study of this pattern because the immigrants have no particular barriers of race prejudice or language to surmount, but they fail anyway. They are two brothers from England, lately-come Imperialists, "nice boys" who work as reporters for a Toronto newspaper. They spend a lot of time talking about the British Empire and writing letters home. After a while they are fired, and for some reason they don't get other jobs; they hang around the newspaper offices until one brother dies and the other disappears. Like Susanna Moodie before them, Callaghan's Bowles brothers can't really settle in. Throughout the story they maintain an attitude of studied remoteness and an enormous capacity for self-deluding make-believe: overlooking Niagara Falls, they compare it to "a cataract in the Himalayas and a giant water-fall in Africa," two places they've never seen. Emotionally they remain tourists, commenting on the ways of the natives in their letters home but unable to fathom them. They make no real contact with the country, nor do they seem to expect anything from it, apart from souvenirs. Reciprocally they make little impact on those who witness the limp spectacle of their failure.

The lack of expectation is a common characteristic of protagonists in Canadian "immigrant" fiction. The characters don't think they are coming to a promised land; as a rule they come to get away from bad conditions somewhere else, but they are not travelling *towards* anything. No Statue of Liberty or Golden Doors await them. When they do have expectations, these are purely material: as Walter Bauer says in his poem "Emigrants," "like a messianic pronouncement / one word was heard again and again: / money." Canada does pretend to offer a promise: she seems to offer newcomers a chance to exploit her; but this promise is seldom kept, at least in fiction. The would-be exploiters become the exploited, as they join the swelling ranks of Canadian victims.

Austin Clarke's collection of short stories, *When He Was Free and Young and He Used To Wear Silks*, is remarkable for the variety of changes it rings on this theme. Here the immigrants are black West Indians. You might expect the stories to be about black-white relationships, and there is a little of this, but the real core of the book seems to be money: the difficulty of obtaining it, the consequences of not having it, the resentment against others who have it – especially European immigrants – and the spiritual price paid by those who get it and their ultimate failure anyway. In two of the stories, "Four Stations in his Circle" and "The Motor Car," the two protagonists are ironically named Jefferson and Calvin, after one of the fathers of American Democracy and the chief architect of the Protestant ethic. Both Jefferson and Calvin labour very hard to acquire the symbols of material success – a house in Rosedale, a car – repudiating their background and race to do so and denying the claims of their relatives and friends "back home." Jefferson won't send any of his precious money to his dying mother, Calvin is ashamed of the postcards he receives from his Black Nationalist buddy. Both of them get the objects they long for, but Jefferson can't afford any furniture for his four-story mansion and Calvin almost wrecks his motor car the first day out. Both want the objects, not to become accepted as equals in their societies (the society of black immigrants they discard, the society of rich white people they admire and hate), but to be applauded as superiors. In both cases the object achieves nothing for them: Jefferson's neighbours think he's the gardener and no one pays any attention to Calvin's motor car. Each object requires a blood sacrifice: Jefferson's mother dies (and he goes mad in his empty house), Calvin's car accident snaps the neck of the white girl riding with him – a girl he's selected not as a person or even a sexual partner but as a decoration for the car.

These two stories of failure masquerading as achievement are balanced by two stories of failure pure and simple, "Waiting for the Postman to Knock" and "Give Us This Day: And Forgive

Us." In both the central characters are out of work, about to be evicted, and outraged by the forces which have somehow failed to provide them with money and which they identify as Canada. Enid, in the first, is "cussing sheself that she ever was foolish enough to say she emigrading to this terrible place called Canada"; Henry, in the second, has as his symbol of failure a Royal Bank of Canada account book in which he writes fabulous sums but which actually contains three dollars. One story in the book appears to display positive sentiments about Canada: the girl Estelle, in "They Heard A Ringing of Bells," waxes positively lyrical about the merits of the country:

> "I am up in this big-able Canada. From a little little village somewhere behind God back I come up here, and now enjoying a little goodness o' life. Little good living that only the white people and the rich black people back home does enjoy. . . ."

But in the context of the story the speeches are ironic: Estelle has only been in Canada a few weeks, she is about to be deported because she can't find work, and her man Sagaboy is dying of tuberculosis.

There are numerous full-length novels which plot the graph of failure, a failure shared by each immigrant regardless of location in Canada or point of origin. The range can be indicated by three: John Marlyn's *Under the Ribs of Death*, with Hungarian immigrants and a Winnipeg setting; Adele Wiseman's *The Sacrifice*, again set in Winnipeg but with middle-European Jewish immigrants; and Brian Moore's *The Luck of Ginger Coffey*, with Irish immigrants and a Montreal setting.

The pattern is clearest in Marlyn's book: the protagonist, Sandor Hunyadi, suffers persecution in childhood because of his origin and the poverty that seems to accompany it, and when he grows up renounces his background, changes his name to Alex Hunter and poses as an "English" Canadian businessman. His new name – with its suggestions of Alexander the Great, conqueror of the world, and of the predatory hunting-and-killing stance Sandor feels success requires – is very important to him, symbolizing as it does a new identity:

> No one started, snickered, or gaped when this name was spoken; it came easily to the tongue. Eyebrows remained in place at its mention. A new name . . . that seemed to absolve him of all he had done in his previous existence.
>
> Looking at it, it was as though he could see the tattered husk of his former self. He felt he had left behind all that was worthless and had been born anew. . . .

In order to make the break he feels compelled to adopt the ruthless attitudes which characterize the commercial world he has entered. He teeters on the brink of wealth, but the Depression catches him short-handed and at the end of the book he finds himself back in poverty again. Two other failure stories parallel his: that of his father, who feels Sandor can achieve "success" – which for him is intellectual or spiritual success – without abandoning the gentle old-world ethic he himself believes in; and that of his Onkel Janos, who sells his soul by marrying a rich old woman he doesn't love and who mutilates him, literally. Neither of these failures is as great as Sandor's – his father retains his integrity though he remains poor, and Onkel Janos breaks away from his evil wife and attains happiness with another woman (though he too must remain poor); Sandor's eventual poverty is without these compensations. Hope for him lies in his baby son, the third generation, and at the end of the book he looks at the child:

. . . He looked into his eyes, so widely and innocently open to his gaze that it shamed him to look so deeply into another human being. Yet he was filled too with a gladness such as he had rarely known; because in those mild depths, it seemed to him, were all those things, miraculously alive, which he had suppressed in himself; stifled for the sake of what he had almost felt within his grasp, out there, over his son's head, out and beyond in the grey desolation.

Perhaps – though it is by no means certain – the third-generation son will be able to reconcile the spiritual values of the first generation and the material ones of the second; though in Marlyn's book the spiritual and the material seem irreconcilable. To enter Canada spiritually is to enter the Death-monster of the title; Alex Hunter, Sandor's Canadian creation, has sold his own soul and failed to gain the world in return.

You will already have noticed the parallel between the three-generational structure of Marlyn's novel and the three-generation patterns we looked at in Chapter Six, and in fact many Canadian immigrant novels cover three generations. But the dynamics of the generations are somewhat different. The first generation in the immigrant novel is typically seen as having more charm and wisdom, or vitality, or cultural suavity, than its WASP counterpart; the second generation has more energy – it really fights for success – and the third generation is given a better chance for a full human life. (Which evokes a picture of the WASP novelists gathered in a group, muttering things like "They'll see" and "Wait till they find out.") The positive qualities of the three immigrant generations are certainly not seen as deriving from Canada; they come instead from the European past. Canada is the background against which they are displayed, the "grey desolation," the land of death. And in the land of death, simply staying genuinely alive – spiritual survival – is a kind of triumph. For instance, Clarke's characters are defined as "failing" to the degree that they enter the melting pot, acquire cars and become "Canadian" – they lose their human vitality and can't enjoy the hardware goodies they get in return.

The three generations are present also in Adele Wiseman's novel *The Sacrifice*. On one level this book is a complex religious allegory, on another a realistic family novel; but on a third it is another immigrant story, and as this it is a long saga of disaster. Abraham and his wife flee Middle Europe, "running from death," after a pogrom in which the two sons, Moses and Jacob (potential prophets and leaders of men) were killed. As Abraham's name indicates, he wishes to be a patriarch, founder of a clan, so the death of his two sons is an obsession with him. His only hope rests with his third son, Isaac, who is the sacrifice – one of them – of the title.

Abraham settles in Winnipeg because it is where the train happens to stop, but he refuses to give up any of the cultural and religious values he has brought with him. Isaac learns English, gets a job which requires him to work on Saturdays, and adopts other "progressive" views. His father fights him every inch of the way: he wants Isaac to be a success, but only on his own terms, not on Isaac's, and certainly not on Canada's. His spiritual error – like that of the WASP patriarchs in Chapter Six – lies in confusing God's will with his own. Isaac dies after a fire in the synagogue during which Abraham's values have taken him over temporarily and he has given himself as a sort of burnt offering in an effort to rescue the Torah. Everyone else in the congregation regards Isaac's act as a miracle; he himself, because of his loss of faith, can view it only as an accident.

After Isaac's death and that of his wife, Abraham becomes more and more withdrawn; finally, in a moment of temporary insanity, he acts out his chosen role by killing an "immoral" woman as a sacrifice to his own idea of the God who has deprived him of his sons. At the end of the book he is in a mental institution. In the last scene he is visited by his grandson, named Moses Jacob after his two dead sons. The grandson has imagined the old man as a demon, a murderer, but when he actually confronts him he feels not hate but love. For the grandson, salvation lies not in rejecting the world of his grandfather, nor in trying to re-create it, but in accepting it as part of his own past. Perhaps he will be able to achieve "success" in Canada's terms without losing the larger spiritual values that the old man has come to represent.

Even though its protagonist ends his days as an insane murderer, *The Sacrifice* closes on a relatively positive note, with the generations reconciled and a future of possibilities made available to the grandson. Wiseman can only project authentic success into the future, not depict it; but the chief obstacles to success – rejecting the new land altogether, and being destructively assimilated by it – do seem to have been effectively worked through in the first two generations. Imaging success for the grandson does not seem – in the book's terms – unrealistic.

It's interesting that *The Sacrifice*, the most optimistic of the novels here discussed, is told largely from the point of view of first-generation Abraham, whereas *Under the Ribs of Death* recounts the story of the second generation. Mordecai Richler's *Son of a Smaller Hero* is another three-generational immigrant novel, but this time the main character is third-generation. The tone of *The Sacrifice* is lyrical, that of *Under the Ribs of Death* is realistic; Richler's novel is almost unrelentingly satirical.

The grandfather here is Melech Adler (translated: King Eagle), a domineering old patriarch with mottled hands and little of Abraham's sweetness. The second generation is represented by his son Wolf, who is predictably obsessed with money and who dies, like Isaac in *The Sacrifice*, trying to rescue a symbol from a fire. Instead of the Torah, the sacred object is a box which he believes to be full of money but which actually contains some scrolls copied from the Torah by Melech. After his death he is ironically proclaimed a hero by the community. But there are secrets: what the religious writings in the box conceal from all but the grandson Noah are some letters and pictures pertaining to Melech's European past, in which he has apparently loved a Gentile girl. Everyone in *Son of a Smaller Hero* has a skeleton in the closet, and Noah, discovering this, decides that his ghetto community has no right to dictate to him the terms of his life. Like Sandor, he searches for an alternative identity in the larger Canadian WASP community, but (of course) doesn't find one. Stuck between the two horns of the dilemma – stay with the ethnic minority and be stifled, assimilate and lose your soul – he gives up trying to make it in Canada and at the book's end takes off for Europe, reviled by all his relatives, who accuse him of running out on them. There is no reconciliation of the generations, though Noah tries for forgiveness; there is however an escape which parallels the escape of the third generation in the WASP novels, and we assume Noah is running off to Europe to become an artist. His name implies he is the only one in his community who has the presence of mind and the moral insight necessary for the construction of a private Ark, which will preserve him against the Canadian Deluge in which the rest of his family will drown. His return to Europe brings the family – much to their disgust – full circle; for Noah, Canada is little more than a place to get out of as quickly as you can. To move beyond failure is to go someplace else.

Brian Moore's *The Luck of Ginger Coffey* approaches the subject from a comic rather than a satiric angle, and rolls all three generations into one, but the essential patterns of failure are still there. Ginger Coffey is not made into a loser by Canada; he was one back in Ireland too. But he comes to the right place: in fiction, Canada stands always ready not only to manufacture and export failure but to attract it and provide for it an appropriate setting. Coffey has mistaken Canada for America: he has renounced static Ireland, hoping to get rich quick. But it hasn't worked, and as the novel opens Coffey has run through first-generation flight from the old country, second-generation failure to achieve material success, and is about to head for Europe like Noah Adler . . . except that he's spent the ticket money. The novel traces his obsessive search for a job that is good enough to match his unrealistic image of himself, paralleled by the gradual deterioration of his marriage. Finally, confronted by yet one more job failure, drunk and revelling in self-pity, titillating himself with images of himself as an outcast, "going into the Arctic night, condemned forever to this land of ice and snow, this hell on earth," he gets caught pissing outdoors and is arrested for committing a public nuisance. During the trial he decides that his hopes and ambitions have been shams, and after it he experiences a moment of ego-free liberation similar to Sandor's as he gazes into the eyes of his child: "He was no one: he was eyes staring at the sky. He was the sky." But his wife and child are restored to him – as a kind of Book of Job reward, the reader feels – and Coffey exits with an almost lyrical tribute to failure:

> Didn't most men try and fail, weren't most men losers? Didn't damn near everyone have to face up someday to the fact that their ship would never come in? . . . He had tried: he had not won. But oh! what did it matter? He would die in humble circs: it did not matter. There would be no victory for Ginger Coffey, no victory

big or little, for there, on the courthouse steps, he had learned the truth. Life was the victory, wasn't it? Going on was the victory . . .

He has learned Canada's lesson well. Endurance, survival, no victory.

The Canadian experience for immigrants seems programmed for failure. A variation of the pattern – Canadians as emigrants – is found in Clark Blaise's story "The Fabulous Eddie Brewster." Here, the setting is America and the immigrants are Canadians: an all-Canadian duo, expansive Louis Broussard from Montreal and his priggish Scottish-descended wife Mildred from Regina. Louis has left Canada and is trying to make his fortune in Florida as a salesman, but success eludes him. After the war his impoverished brother Etienne arrives from France where he settled after the First World War. Etienne achieves the success Louis covets, and he does it by following the American ground rules for immigrants: he changes his name to Eddie Brewster, refuses to speak French but adopts a phoney Maurice Chevalier accent, opens a "French" restaurant, advertises it widely and vulgarly, and packs it full of floor-show attractions and some backroom gambling. Louis could have participated in Eddie's triumph but he won't take the risk, and tight-lipped Mildred disapproves. At the end of the story Eddie has become very wealthy and has been elected mayor. Louis is still a failure, but by now he is a divorced failure. The final revelation is that during the war Eddie collaborated with the Nazis. Success the American way, the story implies, requires collaboration; the Lou-Mildred Canadian duo just don't know how. They can't drop their Canadian identity, their capacity for failure, into the melting pot the way Eddie does.

There's one more piece of "immigrant" fiction that deserves

notice, if only for purposes of comic relief (hardly for those of Canlit courses). It's Marika Robert's novel *A Stranger and Afraid*. Ostensibly it's about the sexual problems of a woman who enjoys being hit with a belt, but en route it contains some fascinating, if not downright repelling, images of Canada as seen through the eyes of an immigrant masochist. Masochistically, she's chosen the wrong country: everyone here is on her side, competing, and she has a rough time scaring up anything that even *looks* like a decent sadist.

Well then. Back in Europe, she knew this absolutely smashing, suave, cultured, competent and dashing sadist named André. But he is killed falling off a horse, so she comes to Canada. All she can dredge up here is a pale grey husband named Neil, and, when he fails to supply the necessary dominance, a total clod – his name, in fact, is Claude – acquired through *Justice Weekly*. Call them Canadians . . . Neil is as soft as Pla-Doh, Claude is a vegetarian and has a swimming pool and some friends who show dirty movies but can't work the projector. He is laconic, barbaric and uncouth, and when he lets his sadism get out of control the heroine knocks him down with a marble bookend. If Canada, land of victims, fails to provide the right kind of suffering, *even for a masochist*, things are tough indeed.

Short List:

CLARKE, Austin, *When He Was Free and Young and He Used To Wear Silks*; AN, $2.95.
MARLYN, John, *Under the Ribs of Death*; NCL, $1.95.
MOORE, Brian, *The Luck of Ginger Coffey*; NCL, $2.35.
WISEMAN, Adele, *The Sacrifice*; Macmillan, Laurentian Library, $1.25.

Long List:

BAUER, Walter, "Emigrants," *Volvox*; Sono Nis.

BLAISE, Clark, "The Fabulous Eddie Brewster," *New Canadian Writing* 1968; Clarke Irwin.

CALLAGHAN, Morley, "The Last Spring They Came Over," WI.

CLARKE, Austin, *When He Was Free and Young and He Used To Wear Silks*; AN.

MARLYN, John, *Under the Ribs of Death*; NCL.

MOODIE, Susanna, *Roughing It in the Bush*; NCL.

MOORE, Brian, *The Luck of Ginger Coffey*; NCL.

RICHLER, Mordecai, *Son of a Smaller Hero*; NCL.

ROBERT, Marika, *A Stranger and Afraid*; Canadian Bestseller Library.

WISEMAN, Adele, *The Sacrifice*; Macmillan, Laurentian Library.

8

THE CASUAL INCIDENT OF DEATH
Futile Heroes, Unconvincing Martyrs and Other Bad Ends

I believe with a perfect faith in all the history
I remember, but it's getting harder and harder
to remember much history.

– *Leonard Cohen,*
"A Migrating Dialogue"

But the mad bomber, Chartier of Major Street, Chartier
said it: that if a country has no past,
neither is it a country and promptly
blew himself to bits in the parliament john, leaving as civil

                                  testament

assorted chunks of prophet, twitching and
bobbing to rest in the flush.
And what can anyone do in this country, baffled and
making our penance for ancestors, what did they leave us?

                         Indian-swindlers,

stewards of unclaimed earth and rootless what does it

                         matter if they, our

forebears' flesh and bone were often
good men, good men do not matter to history.

– *Dennis Lee,*
Civil Elegies

The noise of the images
that are people I will never understand.
Admire them though I may.
Poundmaker. Big Bear. Wandering Spirit,
those miserable men.
Riel. Crazy Riel. Riel hanged.
Politics must have its way.
The way of noise. To fill up.
The definitions bullets make,
and field guns.
The noise your dying makes,
to which you are the only listener. . . .
The images of death hang upside-down.
Grey music.

           – John Newlove,
           "Crazy Riel"

Progressivist historians do not write much about the losers of
history, because belief in progress often implies the base assumption that to lose is to have failed to grasp the evolving truth.
Nevertheless, the losers existed and they are well worth reading
now that we see what kind of society the winners have made.

           – George Grant,
           Technology and Empire

In the last three chapters I've been talking about certain kinds of representative Canadian literary figures, most of which have been "ordinary" people; that is, they are men not different in kind from the society they stand for, they are engaged in occupations defined as normal by that society, and they are not particularly outstanding. In the first section of Chapter Five, however, we looked at the Explorer as a literary concept; I would now like to examine several problems that arise in connection with the literary Hero, more specifically with the attempts to create Heroes based on historical figures. The Explorer of course is a kind of "heroic" figure, but he is not essentially connected with any society or group of people; he is a loner, whereas the Hero has traditionally been the champion of a society, fighting its enemies on its behalf.

Let me elucidate what I mean by "Hero." Imagine a writer who wishes to write something – suppose it is to be a play or a long poem or an opera – in an epic or tragic mode; not a satire, a romance or a comedy. He knows that for the kind of play he has in mind a hero is necessary. His hero must struggle against obstacles, as heroes traditionally do; the struggle must be meaningful, it must have significance for people other than the hero himself, he must be fighting on behalf of his own group or nation. If the hero is allowed to win, his victory must save a people also; St. George defeats the Dragon, Beowulf kills Grendel, Odysseus kicks out the false suitors, and folks can sleep at night. If he has to die, his death must still be in some way redemptive; he must take some of his enemies down with him and help to make a victorious or at least a safe future possible. Traditionally the hero must have a tragic flaw or two; he may be a man destroyed by his own pride, like Oedipus, or by his own indecisiveness, like Hamlet, but he must also have great virtues. Above all he must be central, significant: issues and kingdoms depend on his rise and fall.

Now imagine that this writer is searching for his hero in the twentieth century. The twentieth century alters things: it is the century of Everyman, or so we are told. It does not believe readily in heroes, though it is fond of villains. Our writer must concoct a fictional hero – a rock singer or some such – or he may fall back on historical drama and write a play about Sir Thomas More or Elizabeth the First or Abraham Lincoln or George Washington or Benjamin Franklin; this way he will make a lot of money. His dilemma is not insoluble.

Let us further suppose that our writer is Canadian, and that he wishes to set his drama or poem in Canada. Let's throw caution to the winds and imagine he wants to use real historical material. Now he has problems. These problems are connected with the patterns of Canadian history, and the related and perhaps even resultant patterns of the Canadian psyche. That is, his subject will depend on what kinds of figures are made available to him by his country's history, and his approach to his subject will depend on the habits of thought and feeling made available to him by his culture. What, then, have our writers made of our historical "great men"?

—◄◦►—

The traditional hero is defined by the purpose and quality of his death. The title of this chapter is from Pratt's poem *Brébeuf and his Brethren*; it sums up the Canadian way of death. The American way of death, as demonstrated by both history and literature, is death by violence: assassination, lynching, murder, an upsurge of individual or mass maniacal destructiveness in defiance of law. The defiance of law was itself sanctioned by the Revolution, the overthrow of traditional authority, and Americans have been rebelling against authority ever since: outlaws are heroes.

The English way of death, insofar as there is a single one, is death by history; that scene on the battlefield or in the Tower or on the scaffold, just before the axe falls, appears to be essential to a good English historical movie. Shakespeare was fond of death by history; so was Charles Dickens. Such deaths are seen in the perspective of an interrelated series of social events: clashes of factions and ideals, struggles for power on a monumental scale. Those who die know why they are dying.

The Canadian way of death is death by accident. Death by Nature has been discussed already in Chapter Two; those that drown, freeze or fall off mountains are usually seen as victims, of circumstance or of the environment, both by their authors and by the characters within the poem or novel. The victims may acquire a certain stature by their courage and dignity in the face of death, but the deaths themselves are senseless and accomplish nothing. In *The Bush Garden*, Northrop Frye speaks of such deaths as pointless and useless. But what about cases in which a man, defending an ideal or a social group – that is, under circumstances which ought to give his death "heroic" stature – is killed by other men? Are such deaths any less "accidental," any less "casual," do they have a point, are they useful?

Pratt's *Brébeuf and His Brethren* is the story of an heroic attempt that ends in failure: Brébeuf is tortured and killed, as are many of the other priests; the Mission they have built so laboriously is destroyed, and "the remnant of a nation" staggers back to Québec City. Pratt sees fit to end the poem with a section called "The Martyrs' Shrine," which is a tentative effort to ascribe some sort of positive result to the deaths undergone by the Jesuits: the Mission is rebuilt three hundred years later, the dead rise, more or less, from the grave:

> Near to the ground where the cross broke under the
> > hatchet,

And went with it into the soil to come back at the turn
Of the spade with the carbon and calcium char of the
                                                    bodies,
The shrines and altars are built anew; the Aves
And prayers ascend, and the Holy Bread is broken.

Pratt does all that can be done, but the material he is working
with undercuts any attempt to make Brébeuf's death that of a
traditional hero: we know that the Mission is, in fact, a sort of
tourist attraction, and Brébeuf would probably turn over in his
grave if he could see the end result of his ordeal: is *that* all, we
cannot help asking. It's a bit of an anticlimax. And although the
Indians lost eventually, Brébeuf's death did not save *his* society:
the French Catholics lost too.

There is a similar irresoluteness about the ending of Don
Gutteridge's long narrative poem, *Riel*. Riel is the perfect
all-Canadian failed hero – he's French, Indian, Catholic, revolutionary and possibly insane, and he was hanged by the
Establishment – and as such has inspired a number of works,
among them a play (John Coulter's *The Trial of Louis Riel*) and
an opera, Harry Somers' and Mavor Moore's *Riel*. Gutteridge
writes in the tradition of Pratt, using a similar technique, inter-
spersing original narrative and lyrical passages with historical
documents, some imagined, some real and left intact. In the
symbolism of the poem Riel stands for the authentic life of
the land, Sir John A. Macdonald for the attempt to impose
on the land an artificial structure alien to it, building a "care-
fully contrived nation of blocks." His famous railway is an act
of aggression against the land and the native languages, French
and Indian; it is "straight as a gun-barrel," "a steel tongue
intoning / its single word." Among the "documents" are a letter
from "Sergeant ————," a member of the expedition sent

by Sir John A. against Riel; he experiences difficulties with the journey similar to Brébeuf's camping-trip problems:

> At Lake Superior, not only the shale and boulders of the great cliffs blocked our way, but the pines, hundreds of years old, seemed for no apparent reason to have collapsed across the 'road,' almost as if we were intruders. And for weeks we cut and pulled and dragged our fatigued bones through the most abominable bushland known to man. . . .

These men are in fact intruders; Nature and Riel alike attempt to reject them. But the soldiers and Sir John A. win, the railroad goes through, and "metal" squares and rectangles replace the "wood" and the curved season-shaped natural rhythms of the prairie. (This is, you'll notice, reminiscent of the Settler-versus-Land imagery we noticed in Chapter Five.)

Riel, the man who wished to secede from Sir John's monolithic vision and found a Métis state, falls before an almost faceless authority like an old city block before a highrise developer. "Riel had forfeited his life," Gutteridge quotes from *The Mail*, "and as it valued law and order in the North-West . . . the Administration was bound to make an example of him." Riel is as much a man with a "mission" as is Brébeuf (he thinks of himself as a prophet, he is much obsessed by his adopted middle name, David), and he is seen as a small David battling the Goliath of Ottawa (the metaphor for his resolution is "this flowing: coiled inside, like a smooth stone.") The difference between the Bible and Canada is that in the Bible God helps, miracles happen, David wins. But Riel's defeat is absolute, and unlike Brébeuf he doesn't even get to be a tourist attraction. The poem ends with his death:

Well, the God damned son of a bitch is gone at last!

Yeah, the son of a bitch is gone for certain now.

Along the banks of the ancient Ottawa
The grey towers stand.

This confrontation, individual against the impersonal "grey towers" of the "Administration," authentic people against imposed culture, attempted revolution foiled by the Mounties, is repeated over and over in Canadian history and in the historical narratives based on it.

Not all Canadian history took place in the nineteenth century, but the twentieth century patterns which writers choose – or which history chooses for them – are remarkably similar. A recent and remarkable play, Carol Bolt's *Buffalo Jump*, tells the story of one of Riel's successors-in-spirit, Red Evans (a composite hero based on two historical figures) and his fight against R. B. Bennett, reincarnation of Sir John A., and his Goliath Mounties.

Evans is a union organizer who leads a march through Vancouver and later a railway odyssey across Canada in an attempt to gain improved conditions for relief-camp workers during the Depression. His men make it only as far as Regina, where Bennett orders the Mounties to get them. The confrontation scene between Evans and Bennett, West and East again, could be straight out of *Riel*: while Evans and his delegation are presenting their case, Bennett sits down behind a model of the Parliament Buildings so that his face is hidden. Those grey towers again. The overall shape of the play is Canadian pure and simple: courageous struggle against overwhelming odds, followed by defeat at the hands of an impersonal giant. It's perhaps significant that the only group of people who are nice to the strikers – the citizens of Golden – are played as characters in an operatic farce. Goodness in such a vision is too good to be true. The play ends with the Regina riot, and the last characters on stage are the victorious Mounties.

I believe that in all three of the examples before us there is an uneasiness, an uncertainty of focus, which at its best can be a teasing ambiguity but at its worst is confusion; and although the confusion may have existed on the part of the authors, it will be magnified if the reader approaches these works looking for a "great man" Hero. Here are some tentative suggestions which may indicate, if not the ultimate reasons for these two kinds of confusion, at least their nature.

- *Canadian history defeats attempts to construct traditional society-saving or society-changing heroes.* The imaginative pattern we've been observing is one of useless individual death, coupled with the defeat of the protagonist's society and the absence of social consequence or significance. All Canadian revolutions are failed revolutions, and our writer, searching the past for Hero materials, will find himself almost inevitably writing a drama in which an individual defending the rights of a small group finds himself up against faceless authority – the Establishment, embodied usually by the Mounties – and is overcome by it. His death or defeat does not save his group: Riel is hanged and the Métis perish as a people, Brébeuf dies for his faith and the English Protestants win eventually; the same is true of Dollard and the defence of the Long Sault (see Lampman's poem "At the Long Sault"). William Lyon Mackenzie loses and so does his cause. The two historical moments at which mild congratulation might seem in order – the War of 1812 and the building of the trans-Canada railroad (or, for that, substitute Confederation; both symbolize the unifying of the country) – cannot sustain elation in the face of the irony of history: Canada repels invasion in 1812 and the Yanks take over anyway; Macdonald pulls the country together and now it's about to fall apart.

Canadian history and the Canadian imagination, then, conspire to make a plausible heroic death – a death that accomplishes something, means something in terms of its society – almost impossible. The works of literature built on history reflect this near impossibility, though authors may strain for the desired "traditional" significance. Frequently, however, they bow to the inevitable and write about the Hero-as-loser or -victim, almost despite themselves.

• *Canadians don't know which side they're on.* This remark applies to situations such as those in *Riel* and *Buffalo Jump* in which would-be revolutionaries confront the Mounties and lose. Both of these works suffer from a confusion about the nature and moral position of authority which is in fact a confusion in the Canadian psyche itself. Author and audience sympathies in both cases are with the rebels; but if the rebels had won, what then? Canadians – and not only Canadian Prime Ministers – are terrified of having authority undermined, monolithic federalism shaken. A house divided against itself cannot stand, we mutter endlessly. If the railroad hadn't gone through, the Americans would have got the West; if the country falls apart, who will inherit the pieces?

Canada has from the beginning defined itself as a place where revolutions are really rebellions, against lawful authority – which, as we noted in Chapter Five, is seen as the social form of a divine order. This may work in positive or negative ways (no one riots, for instance, when things like Civil Rights get suspended) but the fact remains that it's hard for Canadians to see the Mounties – symbol of "lawful authority" – as the enemy pure and simple. (Canada must be the only country in the world where a policeman is used as a national symbol; the Canadian contestant in Miss Universe contests invariably wears a cute Mountie uniform. Maybe the only alternative would be a beaver uniform, and dressing up like a Mountie beats dressing up like a peach or a potato, as do Misses Georgia and Idaho; still . . .)

But if the enemy in its lawful authority is not really an enemy but a necessary and mitigated evil, a fact of life, then the construction of "revolutionary" heroes becomes difficult; you get not so much a hero as one who has allowed himself to be a victim of idiot circumstance, like a man who goes swimming in a thunderstorm. The order of the universe, one half of our schizophrenic Canadian consciousness can't help feeling, will of course strike him down.

His death may be a death-by-accident (as befits a Canadian hero), like that of Chartier the mad bomber, who tried to blow up the Parliament Buildings but only succeeded in blowing up himself, by mistake, and, ignominiously, in the john. But the half of the Canadian psyche that distrusts and fears any attempt to overthrow even a repressive authority will see such deaths as proper and meaningful retribution; while the other half, the one which is on the side of the underdog because it identifies with the *victims* of repressive authority, will see the death as pointless because wasted: the death hasn't accomplished

191

the revolution. But then, the first half of the psyche never meant it to. Canadian rebellions have never become revolutions precisely because they have never received popular support. "Prophets" here don't get very far against the Civil Service; which is of course the hidden Clark Kent side of that romantic red-coated collective superhero on the Musical-Ride horse.

• *The attempt to create a traditional individual hero may be misguided in Canada.* Demanding that we have "Heroes" may be like demanding that we have a Frontier of our very own, or like putting down all Canadian books because they aren't *Moby-Dick*: it may be just a symptom of a colonial state of mind. The attempt to write up "great man" Heroism in Canada may parallel the Lake-District-in-Algonquin-Park approach to Nature: insisting that Nature here should be what Wordsworth saw. The "great man" – and possibly also the "anti-hero" and the "representative little man," like Willy Loman in *Death of a Salesman* – may well be foreign models, and outmoded ones at that, which don't grow authentically when transplanted. But the attempt may still break ground, if only by demonstrating that the foreign model doesn't work very well here.

Several critics, including Northrop Frye and Robin Mathews, have suggested that the pull of the native tradition is not in the direction of individual heroes at all, but rather in the direction of collective heroes. This can be seen even in the examples we've chosen. Brébeuf is not the *only* individual to undergo ordeals and martyrdom: there are also the "Brethren," and a lot of the poem's time is spent on them. The spotlight is diffused, not focussed. Similarly, in *Riel* an apparently disproportionate amount of space is given over to the description of a Métis buffalo hunt: it's the people, not just Riel, who exist and resist.

And in *Buffalo Jump* the real "hero" is not Red Evans by himself – he comes through merely as a catalyst – but the men on the march. These collective heroes are as capable of failure as individual ones, and these three examples do in fact fail; the point is that it is they, rather than individual "great men," who are the real emotional focus.

A favourite epic theme has been the building of the railroad across Canada. Pratt has a poem on it, "Towards the Last Spike," and there are Pierre Berton's popular prose treatments, *The National Dream* and *The Last Spike*. Again, building the railroad is not seen as the achievement of a single individual. Sir John A. Macdonald may be a focus, but the railroad is actually *built* by a large group of men, and it is thus that Pratt handles the "heroic" act. The passengers on the Titanic, the seamen of "The Roosevelt and the Antinoe," the men at Dunkirk – these are the collective heroes in three other poems by Pratt. In looking for individual, or individualist, heroes in Canadian literature we may be looking for the wrong thing in the wrong place.

This has obvious literary and social advantages and disadvantages. The collective hero can be an expression of a closed and ingrown garrison mentality or of a living community; collective action has been necessary for survival but it may also stifle individual growth. And in literature, it can generate moments of emotion which are different *in kind* from those generated by individual heroes; the death of a battalion or a shipload is different from the death of a general. The collective hero may also be crucial to any analysis of the "way out" of the Canadian victim situations we've been defining.

———◁◦▷———

Pushed a step further, the Canadian tendency to favour collective heroes rather than individual ones leads to a positive and deliberate undercutting of individual heroics. For instance, the first re-imagined historical moment in Dennis Lee's *Civil Elegies* goes like this:

> . . . casting back I saw
> regeneration twirl its blood and the rebels riding
> riderless down Yonge Street, plain men much
> goaded by privilege – our other origin, and cried
> "Mackenzie knows a word, Mackenzie
> knows a meaning!" but it was not true. Eight hundred-
> odd steely Canadians
> turned tail at the cabbage patch when a couple of bullets
> fizzed
> and the loyalists, scared skinny by the sound of their
> own gunfire,
> gawked and bolted south to the fort like rabbits,
> the rebels for their part bolting north to the pub: the first
> spontaneous mutual retreat in the history of warfare.
> Canadians, in flight.

Here Mackenzie, posing as Hero, fails to deliver the goods, and *both* sides lose – a typically Canadian record, that (ordinarily there's at least *one* winner).

A similar pattern can be found in Roch Carrier's *La Guerre, Yes Sir!* The ostensible "Hero" is a dead man in a coffin. He has died in the Second World War, and the people in his small Québec village believe him to be a glorious military hero, though at home he was a ne'er-do-well. Actually he died by accident: not even an ignominious death, but a silly one. He didn't want to wait in line at the toilet, went behind a bush instead, and was blown up by a stray landmine. But his death does accomplish something: it unites the people of his village in opposition to the English soldiers who are supervising his funeral. They attack the soldiers in an attempt to recapture the coffin, after the soldiers have terminated the wake.

Again neither side wins, exactly. The soldiers depart eventually, carrying the coffin of their own dead Anglais anti-hero, killed by mistake during the skirmish; the villagers have survived. The point is that there is no individual leader or hero: *all* the villagers participate in the fight, even though they've been fighting among themselves earlier. The assumed hero is both dead and a sham; it's the collective that's alive.

——◄◦►——

When you've recognized a pattern or a tradition, the best course is not to bemoan the fact that it is what it is (tough that we can't write *Hamlet*, we aren't the English Renaissance; tough that we can't have American alienated heroes, we go in for collectives) but to explore the possibilities for using that pattern in as many significant ways as possible. For playwrights and directors, I think the possibilities for collective plays about collective heroes are very exciting. (So did Brecht.) There was a play put on in Toronto in 1972, *Fanshen* by Rick Salutin, which was about the Chinese Revolution and the necessity for the revolution's being made by all the individuals in the society, working together. The play wasn't just about China.

Short List:

BOLT, Carol, *Buffalo Jump*; Playwright's Co-op, $2.50.
GUTTERIDGE, Don, *Riel*; Van Nostrand Reinhold, $2.95.

PRATT, E. J., *Brébeuf and His Brethren*; Macmillan, $0.95. Also *Selected Poems*; Macmillan, $1.95.

PRATT, E. J., *Towards the Last Spike*; Macmillan. Also *Selected Poems*; Macmillan, $1.95.

Long List:

BERTON, Pierre, *The Last Spike*; M&S.

BERTON, Pierre, *The National Dream*; M&S.

BOLT, Carol, *Buffalo Jump*; Playwright's Co-op.

CARRIER, Roch, *La Guerre, Yes Sir!*; AN.

COULTER, John, *The Trial of Louis Riel*; Oberon.

FRYE, Northrop, *The Bush Garden*; AN.

GUTTERIDGE, Don, *Riel*; Van Nostrand Reinhold.

LAMPMAN, Archibald, "At the Long Sault," *Poets of the Confederation*; NCL.

LEE, Dennis, *Civil Elegies*; AN.

PRATT, E. J., *Brébeuf and His Brethren*; Macmillan. Also *Selected Poems*; Macmillan.

PRATT, E. J., "The Roosevelt and the Antigone"; *Collected Poems*; UTP.

PRATT, E. J., *Towards the Last Spike*; Macmillan. Also *Selected Poems*; Macmillan.

SALUTIN, Rick, *Fanshen* (not in print).

9

THE PARALYZED ARTIST

This is an ancestral mansion
With neither table nor fire
Nor dust nor carpet.

The perverse enchantment of these premises
Is all in their polished mirrors.

The only pastime possible here
Is to look at oneself day and night. . . .

> – *Anne Hébert,*
> "Manor Life"

―――――

It is possible that he is dead, and not discovered.
It is possible that he can be found some place
in a narrow closet, like the corpse in a detective story,
standing, his eyes staring, and ready to fall on his face.
It is also possible that he is alive
and amnesiac, or mad, or in retired disgrace,
or beyond recognition lost in love. . . .

> – *A. M. Klein,*
> "Portrait of the Poet as Landscape"

―――――

I shall always sit here in this hovel
Weeping perhaps over an old Victorian novel
. . . .
Especially shall I hear that starved cricket
My mind, that thinks a railway ticket
Could save it from its enclosed, cramped quality.
That mind where thoughts float round
As geese do round a pond
And never get out.

– *James Reaney,*
"The Upper Canadian"

I come from a country
of slow and diffident words
of broken rhythms
of unsaid feelings.

Next time I am born
I intend to come
from a different country.

– *Elizabeth Brewster,*
"Gold Man"

S o far we've been talking about the patterns our writers have made from material that can be regarded as (to some extent) historical. Now we've come to some configurations that bring us into the present. This chapter deals with Artists or creative people; that is, the kinds of artists we find populating our literature.

In Chapter Six I talked about the characteristics of the three-generational pattern: rigid Grandparents, grey Parents, and Children who attempt to escape both generations. I also said that "escape" pure and simple was usually impossible; the solution to the Child's dilemma was often seen to involve a coming to terms with the past. One way of coming to terms, making sense of one's roots, is to become a creator, and most artist figures in Canadian fiction are in fact third-generation Children. This chapter is about what happens to them, and, possibly, why.

———◁◦▷———

Let us suppose that a man or woman appears on the face of the earth who for reasons unknown decides to become a serious artist. Let us further suppose that by "artist" we mean a writer of prose fiction, a poet or a painter of pictures (we will leave out composers, sculptors, architects and choreographers for the sake of brevity, though their plight is equally relevant). Let us further suppose that the artist in question is not completely self-enclosed, but sees himself as a man with a vision communicable in words or images which he wishes to make accessible to others; and let us yet further suppose that E. K. Brown is correct when he says, "A great art is fostered by artists and audience possessing in common a passionate and peculiar interest in the kind of life that exists in the country where they live."

Finally, let us suppose that our artist lived in Canada and came to maturity not in the sixties – things *have* changed – but in the twenties, thirties, forties or even fifties of this century. What became of him?

He looked around and found himself in a place where people read, it's true, and looked at pictures, but most of the books they read were imported from England and the States and most of the pictures they looked at were either old Group of Seven or travelling exhibitions from abroad. Usually he found that his own work would be dismissed by sophisticated Canadian critics as "second-rate," "provincial," or "regional," simply for having been produced here; by the unsophisticated it might well have been denounced as immoral. In some decades he might have been mindlessly praised for being "Canadian," in other decades just as mindlessly denounced for the same reason. The situation in either case was impossible.

He discovered that the outlets for his work were few: not many galleries, and those depended heavily on imports (that after all is what people buy); not many publishing companies, and those few did a lot of distribution for foreign companies and were notoriously unwilling to take risks on anything new or "experimental," or anything else for that matter. If he was lucky enough to acquire an American or English publisher he might get some attention from the Canadian *literati* and thus from a more widespread audience; but in order to do that he would have to squeeze his work into shapes that were not his, prune off anything "they" might not understand, disguise himself as a fake American or Englishman. At this point he either gave up in disgust (Canada has a high percentage of one-book writers) and became a stockbroker like Dad wanted anyway (artists are a dubious lot, and not much money in it), left the country and headed for one of the "centres of culture" – London, New York or Paris – or stayed and tried to follow his own vision as best he might, knowing that he could expect, at the very best, publication in a slender edition of five hundred copies for poetry and a couple of thousand for novels; at the worst, total oblivion. His plight was exactly that described by E. K. Brown in his important 1943 essay. "The Problem of a Canadian Literature." He experienced full force what members of other professions, such as dentistry, might experience only peripherally: what it means to be living in a cultural and economic colony.

As Hugh MacLennan summed it up in a book of essays, "Boy Meets Girl in Winnipeg: Who Cares?"

It's heartening to realize that the Canadian condition is not unique. Anyone checking through American literary magazines – the few there were – in the decades immediately following the American Revolution, when the U.S. was still a cultural colony though no longer a political one, will find the same complaints, as well as the breast-beatings and searches for the "true" national identity that so often accompany them. Why is there no American Sir Walter Scott, no great American painter, and so forth. It's noteworthy that when the great American writers did come along they weren't recognized till long after their deaths: Americans were too busy reading Charles Dickens.

E. K. Brown offers some further comments on the state of mind of the colonialized audience:

. . . a colony lacks the spiritual energy to rise above routine, and . . . it lacks this energy because it does not adequately believe in itself. It applies to what it has standards which are imported, and therefore artificial and distorting. It sets the great good place not in its present, nor in its past nor in its future, but somewhere outside its own borders, somewhere beyond its own possibilities.

If Brown is right, there are two factors involved in the production of a "great art": the artist and the audience. The artist acts as vision or tongue, giving shape to patterns in which the audience may then recognize itself, for better or worse: "identify" itself. Take away the artist and the audience can never achieve self-knowledge. If we are to believe Shelley, the artist is both representative man and leader; in his work is made visible all that is best and worst in a society. He is us.

But take away the audience, and the artist has part of himself cut off. He is blocked, he is like a man shouting to no one. Without a sense of his audience he can have no ultimate sense of purpose, no feeling that what he produces has any significance. He may also find himself with nothing to write about except himself. He might as well be living on the Moon. He is a man talking to himself, and talking to oneself is usually considered either a result of isolation or a symptom of insanity.

A. M. Klein's poem "Portrait of the Poet as Landscape" is an examination of the artist's position in a society from which – for whatever reasons – he is cut off, and of the effects his invisibility may be expected to have on his work. The poem begins by wondering if the poet is dead, then reveals he's not dead "but only ignored":

> The truth is he lives among neighbours, who, though
>   they will allow
> him a passable fellow, think him eccentric, not solid,
>   a type that one can forgive, and for that matter, forego.

The "neighbours," the audience, do not believe in the reality or importance of what the poet is doing, and their lack of belief creates a corresponding lack in himself; he is "everywhere menial, a shadow's shadow." His only audience is other poets, and this produces an inbred, distorted art, a concentration on technique for its own sake. "Schizoid solitudes," Klein calls them; the attitude of their society isolates them, makes them introverts, "set apart . . . . as on a reservation."

When "Portrait of the Poet as Landscape" is placed beside another poem by another poet equally bent on investigating the conditions of his own world, James Reaney's "The Upper Canadian," another aspect of the poet's cultural isolation appears. The speaker is afflicted with both claustrophobia and fear of the "outside." Canada is like a pond, where the geese sail "in continual circles" and "never get out." There is no viable cultural life in this pond; the speaker can have contact with other writers, but they are all dead and English: he sits "by an empty stove" reading Shakespeare, which he will never see acted. "Culture" is not something that is being created around him: it is something great and dead, entombed in books, inaccessible. It is not only his audience that has been denied him, it is his own culture, in which he might otherwise participate. Klein's poet, being urban, at least knows other artists, weird though they may be; Reaney's is completely isolated.

We speak of isolated people as being "cut off," but in fact something has been cut off from them; as artists, deprived of audience and cultural tradition, they are mutilated. There are various ways of being mutilated. If your arm or leg has been cut off you are a cripple, if your tongue has been cut off you are a mute, if part of your brain has been removed you are an idiot or an amnesiac, if your balls have been cut off you are a eunuch or a *castrato*. There are three novels, all of them significant works of art, all of them dealing with the situation of the artist trying to function in Canadian society, in each of which the artist figure is, emotionally, just such a cripple, mute or castrated man. In none of them is he able to produce any credible art: as an artist, and necessarily then as a man, he is paralyzed, frozen, the equivalent of the stiff corpses that litter the winter landscape in stories about Nature the Monster. The corpses have suffered physical death at the hands of an indifferent or hostile Nature, the artists have suffered emotional and artistic death at the hands of an indifferent or hostile audience.

Philip Bentley in Sinclair Ross's *As For Me and My House* is just such a warped artist (as his last name suggests). In youth he was determined to be a great painter, and various "realistic" reasons are advanced for his failure to become one: he was poor, he entered the Church to make money, thereby compromising himself, Mrs. Bentley came along and he married her, thereby trapping himself economically. When we first meet him he is a preacher in a small, narrow prairie town ironically called "Horizon." He is unable to act or even love. He spends most of his time in his study with the door shut, drawing tight, dead little pictures of stores with false fronts and defeated, faceless people. The pictures are emblems of himself, his entrapment and sense of failure. Nothing works for him: his marriage is lifeless, he's been unable to produce even a child, he hates his work and himself, there's no one with whom he can communicate. Even his dog (called, significantly, El Greco) gets lured away and killed by coyotes, and it isn't too fanciful to see in the fate of the dog a symbol of his own: the society he has to operate in, composed mostly of tiny yapping people with small minds and sharp teeth, has destroyed him. His artistic sterility has its echo in another character in the book, Paul, who treats English as though it were a dead language; he's obsessed with word derivations, and pays more attention to them than to what people are actually saying.

Philip does a little better as the book goes on: he paints the prairie rather than the false store-fronts and these paintings have more vital energy, he fathers a son by a girl who (of course) dies, he quits the ministry with the prospect of running (of course) a *second-hand* bookstore, there is hope that his marriage will improve (though not much hope). But he will never be a great painter, not just because, as Mrs. Bentley, who is nothing if not repetitive, keeps saying, he has no belief in himself, but because Horizon and the culture-at-large it represents is not the sort of place in which great painters are offered roots or are even imaginable. There is a brief but revealing moment towards the end of the book: Mrs. Bentley takes Philip's best paintings and drawings and spreads them out for Philip to view. She's trying to convince him yet once again that he can do it: "Be detached and fair," she says. "Isn't there something there that's important?" Philip makes a deprecating remark. "I gathered them up then," says Mrs. Bentley, "and trying to laugh, said the exhibition was closing for lack of an appreciative public." Exactly.

Another man with a similar problem is David Canaan in Ernest Buckler's *The Mountain and the Valley*. David has aspirations as a writer, and as his name implies he ought to be both the champion and the incarnation of his culture, "David" suggesting the Biblical giant-killer and king, and "Canaan," a most unusual name in Nova Scotia, arrival in the Promised Land, the place where locale and people belong to one another. His father's name is Joseph, and though Buckler doesn't go quite so far as to call his mother Mary (she's Martha instead), the stronger, protective older brother is named Christopher, after Saint Christopher the Christ-bearer. David is also supposed to be a sort of Christ, redeeming his people. "His people" are the inhabitants of Entremont, its French name indicating its situation *between* the mountains. As in Tennyson and the Bible, "mountain" is the place of vision; "valley" the scene of ordinary daily life. David's people are in exile, unredeemed, because they have no language equal to the full expression of life and emotion: they are inarticulate, emotional deaf-mutes, unable to "tell" each other anything, unable to "look in the eye" of their "own watching." They rarely feel the lack of this capacity, which David possesses. With his gift of speech he might perform the function of artist, "articulate" the community so it could become visible to itself.

But the champion fails. He is regarded as something of a freak by the members of his family, "different," a little maimed; an attitude that becomes a prophecy when he falls from a barn rafter and injures his head. His first love dies young and no one replaces her, he does not marry; he is unable to escape, join the larger world of cities and wars where he dreams he might achieve self-realization; and the mountain accords him its vision only at the moment before his death (at the age of thirty, of a mysterious seizure). As a child he has planned to build a camp at the top of the mountain and write a book in it. He never does, and the integrating, synthesizing act that would have unified place, people, language and time, "inside" and "outside," dies with him. For some reason his author cannot leave him alive with his book even a future possibility, as it is for Stephen Dedalus at the end of Joyce's *Portrait of the Artist as a Young Man*. A great writer, an artist of any kind, is not imaginable in Entremont.

Entremont and Horizon, though, are a long way from "cultural centres," and a distance back in time. What of places where education is at least available and art is not a foreign word? London, Ontario, for instance, in the late fifties or early sixties, the setting of Graeme Gibson's novel *Five Legs*. Surely chances should be better here?

Not so. Almost every character in the book is a thwarted writer, and it's made evident that the fault is just as much that of the culture, the potential audience, as it is that of the flawed psyches of the individual characters. Of the three main characters, Lucan, Martin and Felix, two have already made choices which have inevitably doomed them to failure both as artists and as men: both have chosen the values of their society rather than the values they should have chosen to actualize themselves as writers. Lucan has chosen a job at a university rather than an insecure sojourn in Europe with the woman he loved and who was about to bear his child. He has married instead a woman who shares the fate of Mrs. Bentley: she is barren. Martin has also hesitated between two women, one offering sensuality and freedom and escape from the responsibilities of his society, the other offering integration with that society. Just after proposing to the second he is killed in a car accident, but his choice indicated that he was already irremediably crippled as a potential artist: he would have turned into Philip Bentley.

For the third character, Felix, there is still hope, though it is a slim hope. He has not yet committed himself to anyone or anything; he has not impregnated anyone or proposed to anyone, in fact he has dodged the issue altogether by refusing to have sexual intercourse at all. His technique for avoiding the fates of Lucan and Martin, for keeping his integrity, is flight, and he flees, one after the other, various women, his family, and the representatives of his society gathered at Martin's funeral; but his flight is not towards anything, it is simply away. The society described, which is like Horizon society with a few frills and pretensions, magnified and distorted nightmarishly, cannot offer him an acceptable model. There are no successful artists in it, though there are a few Bohemian drones and sad old bores; other than that there are only a lot of aggressive and self-righteous businessmen. There is some talk of art, but it is mostly in the form of pretentious dabbling or envious derogatory sneers, or, worse, in the audience's attempt to impose its own starved and bloodless standards on the artist.

At the end of *Portrait of the Artist as a Young Man*, Stephen Dedalus flees from Ireland, another culturally unhealthy climate, to the continent, intending to become a writer. At the end of *Five Legs*, Felix flees into the snow; we don't know what he will become. In *Ulysses* we meet Stephen again: he is becoming a writer. In *Communion* we meet Felix again: he has become an emotional cripple, practically incapable of talking, almost incapable of acting, and certainly incapable of love. Stephen writes poems. Felix gets himself burned up by a clutch of juvenile American delinquents.

Before Felix departs from the funeral in *Five Legs* he has an interesting conversation with Lucan. Lucan, the university professor, has found out somehow that Felix the student has been doing some writing, and Lucan the thwarted writer indulges in some patronizing:

> "Difficult, yes." Rocking he bends, he smiles with laughter in the room. "Particularly in Canada it seems," what? "Have you read, do you know Brown's essay?" He doesn't wait. "A sound analysis, it seems. Rather helpful. Yes. Its difficult alright and he suggests, well. The problems of a real Canadian literature." Sudden silence.

Felix doesn't know the piece (though Gibson obviously does), and Lucan goes on to explain:

> "Goddamn Puritan mentality doesn't simply you know, inhibit the development of naturalism or anything, no! It fears, that's the thing, it demeans the very role of art itself!"

Coming from Lucan, this is no doubt special pleading, an attempt to blame his environment for his own lack of talent; and there's some suggestion that artistic stasis, in Gibson's novel at least, is willed as well as imposed: as long as you can fail to produce, and can blame that failure solely on your culture, you need never be judged by the standards of excellence, or indeed by any standards at all. But though Lucan is whining, Felix is quite genuinely paralyzed by his society; and the will to lose is, for him, not an easy out but a correlative of that society.

The horns of the dilemma, then, as defined by Ross, Buckler and Gibson, are: stay in the culture and be crippled as an artist; or escape into nothing. These are the choices for the characters in their books. The authors themselves had a third choice: write from the centre of the dilemma. Articulating the problem won't solve it, but it will at least make it visible to the community whose problem it is.

There are two documents which should perhaps be read in connection with these studies of destroyed artists. Neither is a novel, both are personal records, journals. One comes from Québec, where the problems facing the artist have been similar, involving possibly more claustrophobia (see for instance Anne Hébert's airtight poems) and, on the part of the audience, less indifference but more moralizing censorship. The other comes from the heartland of WASP Canada. The first is *The Journal of Saint-Denys-Garneau*; the second Scott Symons' *Place d'Armes*. They are both records of suffering inflicted on the individual by cultures too small for the men contained in them. Garneau is meticulous, restrained, forcing himself towards an unattainable ideal of spiritual perfection; Symons throws words at the wall (a reversal of the usual stereotype of clip-lipped *anglais* and effervescent Gallic temperament), or rather, all over Canada, in a kind of hysterical explosion forced by too tight a space:

. . . constrained, constipated, congealed. I can't give in, I can't get out, I can't withdraw, nor proceed. . . . Impasse! Absolute impasse! But I shall – if I have to blast my way. . . .

Symons links sexual inadequacies with cultural ones when he speaks of the great Canadian institution, the civil servant, as "the gelded Canadian who makes a career out of his self-castration in the Ottawa Pork Barrel." For Symons, breaking out of the cultural impasse involves breaking out of the sexual one as well (another spokesman for this equation is of course Irving Layton), and this means also the recovery of the ability to speak, to say, to violate the verbal taboos, language barriers erected by the "Puritan mentality." For this task – the rejection of the role of cripple, the recovery of the full range of human possibilities – the culture has not prepared him; and the task itself is made possible only by desperation.

And then, starting to say it all, there is no structure for expressing it. I was trained to read novels – not to write them! So I start, arrant amateur – to exculpate my culture through the written word – a century behind.

Moreover how can a well-heeled, well-bred, well-educated pampered Canadian complain?

The answer is that my culture is about to die. . . .

———◇———

What to do then?

The solution, for some, has been escape, leaving a country in which it seems impossible to sustain oneself as an artist. Given that the Canadian artist is frozen, paralyzed, does flight unfreeze him? "If you just hole up in Canada," says James Reaney in

"The Canadian Poet's Predicament," "and refuse to educate yourself you are going to be provincial. But if you flee the country, cut yourself off from your roots, you may end up not even being that."

P. K. Page has a poem called "The Permanent Tourists" which suggests some of the consequences of cultural exile:

> Somnolent through landscapes and by trees
> nondescript, almost anonymous,
> they alter as they enter foreign cities –
> the terrible tourists with their empty eyes
> longing to be filled with monuments.

The tourists are empty and lack identity; chameleon-like, they take on the colours of their surroundings, but they have none of their own.

For those who leave, the question of audience remains primary; will they write to be read by their own people, or for the new, foreign audience? If for the latter, they can hope only to be second-rate imitators in their adopted culture. If they can succeed in emptying their heads of Canada, they will in fact be empty, they will be "Permanent Tourists," and the "monuments" they long for can never take genuine root in them. They can use exile as a vantage point, a "mountain" from which to view their own authentic culture, and that may work for a while; but the "valley" that can be seen from such a mountain will always be *only* in the past, and the past, sooner or later, runs out. It is interesting that the only Canadian character in Mordecai Richler's *Cocksure* is a transplanted Canadian, and he is impotent. The transplanted Canadians in another Richler book, *St. Urbain's Horseman*, are worrying about whether leaving was in fact the right choice.

An exiled artist who manages to make it, sort of, is the painter Pierre in Gabrielle Roy's *The Hidden Mountain*. Like David in *The Mountain and the Valley* he has a vision of integration, and he is able to paint at least some of it before his premature death. He has left Canada and gone to Paris, but the pictures he struggles over are not Parisian; they are visions of his own country. Leaving the country cannot give one either another real audience or another "reality" to make art from; but it may alleviate the claustrophobia somewhat, relieve the warping pressures of indifference or too-narrow audience demand, give some space. Some try for both; a number of Canadian writers have spent their lives flying in and out of the country like migrating geese, perhaps because they saw the only other choices as a state of permanent tourism or a static life in the closed circle of the Upper Canadian pond.

—◅o▻—

But perhaps staying and being maimed or leaving and being rootless are no longer the only alternatives. There are other possibilities. One has to do with the distinction between "artist" as a character in a book, and the writer who creates that character. Another has to do with changes in the audience itself.

The first point may seem like quibbling but in fact it's crucial. The paradox that confronts us is that Ross, Buckler and Gibson have created memorable works of art out of the proposition that such a creation, in their environment, is impossible. They are Position Three writers naming the conditions of Position Two, making art out of their characters' inability to do so. The true "symptom" or "reflection" of the limited Calvinist-Colonialist environments they are talking about would be no books at all. Books about artists who are unable to create are, instead, explorations or depictions. One possibility, then, is to write with freedom about blocked writers.

Another possibility relates to the recent expansion (one can't call it a renaissance) in Canadian writing; it's a change in audience, and therefore a change for writers.

In A. M. Klein's poem the poet is anonymous, unrecognized; yet he is re-creating the world like God and naming it like Adam:

> . . . Look, he is
> the nth Adam taking a green inventory
> in world but scarcely uttered, naming, praising . . .

This is an "illusion," but only as all art is an illusion. Klein's poet has to perform his trick in secret; he lives still in the climate described by E. K. Brown. But at the beginning of the sixties it became possible for Canadian poets to acquire an audience not only larger *in ratio* than poetry audiences in the United States, but sometimes larger *in actual numbers*; and though the same will probably never be quite true for fiction writers, serious fiction at the beginning of the seventies is undergoing the same expansion, in terms both of markets and of the writing itself, that poetry did in the sixties.

Publishers are more disposed to publish and distribute Canadian books, though the book market is still largely foreign-dominated. Canada is more willing to look at itself through the vision of its writers, and there has been a corresponding thaw in the artists; they no longer need feel that they are talking to themselves in a room full of deaf people, or living on an island from which they throw bottles with furtive messages, or shining, like Klein's poet, "At the bottom of the sea." They are freer to concentrate on their job, articulating the community, or (to put it another way) creating satisfying structures out of the materials at hand. However, other artists – dramatists and filmmakers, for instance – who are now trying to work in their own country, find themselves undergoing roughly the same kinds of limiting and discouraging experiences previously undergone by writers.

The vision David Canaan has at the end of *The Mountain and the Valley* is not of God and the Angels, nor even of nightclubs in New York. It is a vision of Entremont, the Valley, and the people in it, in all their complexity and limitation. David cannot actualize this vision (though Buckler does); but it is the realization that *this*, all along, was what he ought to have been writing about that is for him the revelation.

In Alice Munro's *Lives of Girls and Women*, there's a more recent treatment of the theme we've been discussing. Again the protagonist, Del Jordan, has secret ambitions as a writer, again the culture is bent on stunting or destroying them, and the situation is compounded by the fact that the potential artist is a woman. She defies the culture, leaves it, and survives to become an artist; but she transfers her imaginative allegiance from the stylized world of Gothic grotesques she has dreamed up as an adolescent to the small-town "here" she despised when she was actually living in it. She chooses to write from the centre of her own experience, not from the periphery of someone else's, and she sees her act of creation as an act of redemption also. It is the "green inventory" she is after, the expression of the hitherto unexpressed: naming the world. "I would try to make lists," Del says:

> The hope of accuracy we bring to such tasks is crazy, heartbreaking.
>
> And no list could hold what I wanted, for what I wanted was every last thing, every layer of speech and thought, stroke of light on bark or walls, every smell,

pothole, pain, crack, delusion, held still and held together –
radiant, everlasting.

This vision is much like Buckler's, much like Klein's, but the
speaker does not die and she does not regard herself as maimed
or invisible. She is a functioning artist, and she is plausible.

Short List:

BUCKLER, Ernest, *The Mountain and the Valley*; NCL, $2.50.
GIBSON, Graeme, *Five Legs*; AN, $2.50.
ROSS, Sinclair, *As For Me and My House*; NCL, $1.50.

Long List:

BROWN, E. K., "The Problem of a Canadian Literature," *Contexts of
Canadian Criticism* (ed. Eli Mandel); UTP.
BUCKLER, Ernest, *The Mountain and the Valley*; NCL.
GIBSON, Graeme, *Communion*; AN.
GIBSON, Graeme, *Five Legs*; AN.
KLEIN, A. M., "Portrait of the Poet as Landscape," *Poets Between the
Wars* (ed. Milton Wilson); NCL.
MUNRO, Alice, *Lives of Girls and Women*; R.
PAGE, P. K., "The Permanent Tourists," *Cry Ararat!*; M&S.
REANEY, James, " The Upper Canadian," *Selected Poems*; N.
RICHLER, Mordecai, *Cocksure*; M&S.
RICHLER, Mordecai, *St. Urbain's Horseman*; M&S.
ROSS, Sinclair, *As For Me and My House*; NCL.
ROY, Gabrielle, *The Hidden Mountain*; OP.
SAINT-DENYS-GARNEAU, *The Journal* (trans. John Glassco); M&S.
SMITH, A. J. M. (ed.), *Masks of Fiction*; NCL.
SYMONS, Scott, *Place d'Armes*; M&S.

10

ICE WOMEN VS EARTH MOTHERS
The Stone Angel and the Absent Venus

. . . old mother North America with her snow hair, her mountain forehead, her prairie eyes, and her wolf teeth, her wind song and her vague head of old Indian memories.

– *Warren Tallman,*
"Wolf in the Snow"

. . . stones
made this country. This country makes us stones.

– *Phyllis Webb,*
"Beachcomber"

They saw her as an incredible crone
The spirit of neglected fence corners,
Of the curious wisdom of brambles,
And weeds, of ruts, of stumps and of things despised.

– *James Reaney,*
One-Man Masque

Dear God, she said, The country. The wilderness. Nothing. Nothing but old women waiting.

– *Sheila Watson,*
The Double Hook

But she lies dumb
Ice and fire die tepid on her tongue
Scorched with cold, the unbeliever
Resists her saviour.

– Anne Wilkinson,
"The Pressure of Night"

What's packed about her ivory bones
Is cruel to the wondering touch;
Her hard skull rounds the roots of stones
And cannot give or comfort much;

Her lap is sealed to summer showers,
Ice-bound, and ringed in iron hold:
Her breast puts forth its love like flowers
Astonished into hills of cold.

Not here the Sun that frees and warms,
Cherishes between fire and flood:
But far within are Seraph forms,
Are flowers, fountains, milk, blood.

– Jay Macpherson,
"The Caverned Woman"

I remember wondering, after first reading Margaret Laurence's novel *The Stone Angel*, why most of the strong and vividly-portrayed female characters in Canadian literature are old women. If you trusted Canadian fiction you would have to believe that most of the women in the country with any real presence at all are over fifty, and a tough, sterile, suppressed and granite-jawed lot they are. They live their lives with intensity, but through gritted teeth, and they are often seen as malevolent, sinister or life-denying, either by themselves or by other characters in their books.

Or, to approach it from another direction: Robert Graves, in *The White Goddess*, divides Woman into three mythological categories or identities. First comes the elusive Diana or Maiden figure, the young girl; next the Venus figure, goddess of love, sex and fertility; then the Hecate figure, called by Graves the Crone, goddess of the underworld, who presides over death and has oracular powers. In Graves' mythology, the three phases together constitute the Triple Goddess, who is the Muse, the inspirer of poetry; she is also Nature, a goddess of cycles and seasons. Hecate, the most forbidding of the three, is only one phase of a cycle; she is not sinister when viewed as part of a process, and she can even be a Wise Old Woman like Ethel Wilson's Mrs. Severance in *Swamp Angel*. But Hecate does become sinister when she is seen as the only alternative, as the whole of the range of possibilities for being female.

It's a good deal more complicated than this, but holding just this simple outline up against Canadian literature we notice some curious things. Diana-Maidens often die young. There is a notable absence of Venuses. And there is a bumper crop of sinister Hecate-Crones. What can account for this? Where do all the Crones come from? They seem to appear fully aged out of nowhere, having skipped two of the usual phases of the Triple Goddess.

223

Or, to put it yet another way: Why are there no Molly Blooms in Canadian literature? Some wag may remark that there are no Molly Blooms in Canada, but there were no Molly Blooms in James Joyce's Ireland either. Molly is a literary creation, finally a metaphor which equates woman and earth-life-cycle process – she is the Idea of Venus, so to speak. The question we must ask is why no Canadian writer has seen fit – or found it imaginable – to produce a Venus in Canada.

One answer may come from Graves's thesis that the Triple Goddess is not only the Muse but also Nature. Simone de Beauvoir and others after her have objected to the tendency in literature to make Woman-Nature metaphors or equations. Their objections are based on the kinds of limiting mystiques about women such metaphors foster, and are no doubt legitimate within certain boundaries; but these are the kinds of patterns literature makes – literature created by women as well as men – and in literature itself they cannot be avoided. Let us suppose then that Woman is Nature, or Nature is a woman. Obviously the kinds of female figures that can be imagined will then depend on what kind of place you live in – a desert is not the same as a jungle – and also on what you think of the kind of place you live in. Some find deserts beautiful and mysterious, others find them hot, sterile and arid.

Nature as woman keeps surfacing as a metaphor all over Canadian literature, and in unlikely as well as likely places. The quotation from Warren Tallman at the front of this chapter about "old mother North America" is from a critical essay, and provides a useful key: Nature is a woman, but an old, cold, forbidding and possibly vicious one. This of course fits into the Nature as Monster theme we looked at in Chapter Two. E. J. Pratt has a female Nature in *Towards the Last Spike*, where he personifies the Canadian Shield as a "thing," not exactly human but at least female, a sort of reptile made of rocks:

This folded reptile was asleep or dead:
So motionless, she seemed stone dead – just seemed:
She was too old for death, too old for life,
For as if jealous of all living forms
She had lain there before bivalves began
To catacomb their shells on western mountains.
Somewhere within this life-death zone she sprawled,
Torpid upon a rock-and-mineral mattress. . . .

The mattress image conjures up a grotesque Marilyn Monroe lolling passively on a couch, and in fact it is the reptile's passivity – her mute stolid resistance – which is the greatest obstacle to the railroad builders driving their tiny phallic spikes into her. But notice the extreme age, the state of being neither alive nor dead, the "jealousy" of "living forms." In Graves's terms this is Nature in her Hecate or world-of-the-dead incarnation, in a special Canadian pink-granite form.

Sometimes the Canadian Nature-goddess is rock, sometimes she is ice, as, for instance, in two poems, one by Earle Birney, one by Gwen MacEwen. Both poets combine Diana and Hecate, virgin and death-goddess; Venus is absent. Almost exactly the same image is used by each. In the Birney poem, "The Mammoth Corridors," the poet awaits the second coming of someone he calls "that madcap virgin mother of ice," who lies "hoarding her cold passion," waiting to "lust back wider than Europe and Pacific deep / bringing her love the rounded silence / a long hard peace." Birney is playing with words as usual, punning on "ice-cap" and "mad," dallying as well with a conceit in which the "virgin mother," who in Christianity is the mother of Christ the Saviour, is in Canada the mother of nothing but ice. But the gigantic goddess he evokes, personification of the next Ice Age, is interesting: she is a sort of Iron Maiden, whose embrace means death. The word "peace" is ironic: the land will be peaceful only because frozen.

In the MacEwen poem, *Terror and Erebus*, this enormous destructive ice virgin makes another appearance, this time as a personification of "the giant virginal strait of Victoria," seen as female by the brooding, doomed explorers of the Franklin expedition:

> But perhaps she might not yield,
> She might not let you enter, but might grip
> And hold you crushed forever in her stubborn loins,
> Join you finally to her horrible house,
> Her white asylum in an ugly marriage. . . .

Here again is the female Nature, union with whom means not life but death, an "ugly marriage" in which the bodies of the explorers become one with the land by being frozen into it. Again she is ornamented with images of madness – her house is an "asylum" – and of a sterile virginity.

In his essay "The Canadian Poet's Predicament" James Reaney talks about "The Canadian Grendel or troll-wife, whose recognition and conquest automatically make a story"; he identifies the troll-wife with the landscape, "the wastes of snow, the hemlock with the acquisitive curl to its gnarled old root . . ." Many poets have evidently agreed with him that the conquest of or defeat by this old female horror are fit subjects for narrative and an appropriate basis for metaphor. Nature, in many Canadian versions, is a nasty chilly old woman.

Poets incline towards Nature-as-woman metaphors; prose writers turn the metaphor around and use Woman-as-Nature. A Canadian novelist whose work comes close to being poetry – that is, to being metaphor – is Sheila Watson. In her novel

The Double Hook, Nature-as-woman and Woman-as-Nature are equally balanced, in the person of a dead old woman who haunts the living characters as a ghost or death goddess. While still "alive" she has in fact been dead; she has dominated those around her and has denied them life, their own existence – the cows, we are told, would turn "their living flesh from her as she'd turned hers from others" – and her ghost is seen by the living characters in the novel fishing in the river, "with a concentrated ferocity as if she were fishing for something she'd never found." The old lady has been killed by her son James in a desperate bid on his part for freedom, but her control remains until the attitudes towards the environment she stands for can be destroyed also. What her ghost represents to those who see it is fear, "Laying traps for men . . . Fear skulking round. Fear walking round in the living shape of the dead."

That it is not fear of death but fear of life is made clear by the fate of Greta, the old lady's daughter, who inherits her place in the house, her chair, and her personality. Greta poses as Venus, in a flowered dressing gown,

> . . . like a tangle of wild flowers grown up between them. All green and gold and purple in the lamplight. Fat clinging lumps of purple flowers. Honey-tongued. Bursting from their green stems. Crowding against green leaves.

But beneath all this lush vegetation she is really the destructive barren ice-goddess. "The same old Greta," another character comments, "inside some plants and bushes." (Externally Greta is young, but the character is right in calling her "old.") Greta wishes to shut out all intrusion from the outside, including other people, love, and the "birth" half of the natural process embodied by the girl who is pregnant by her brother James. She thinks by doing so she will have "peace," but this peace would be the peace of death, as in Birney's poem. When it becomes evident that the outside world will impinge on her despite her shut doors, she burns down the old lady's house, with herself in it. "Greta had inherited destruction like a section surveyed and fenced," another character thinks, making the connection between fences, enclosure, and the negativity of Greta's life.

While alive, the old lady's sin has been her refusal to accept life whole, the "darkness" along with the "light," the cyclical process of Nature as well as man's structures, houses and straight lines. The "something she'd never found" is her own completeness. Her ghost is an after-image; as ghost she is not necessarily evil, but the characters' attitudes towards her can have life-denying consequences for *them*. When the old lady's house – her past and the past she has imposed on others – has been destroyed, her ghost is released from its obsessive search and she is converted from a death-goddess to something like the first stage in a new cycle, a rebirth. She is last seen standing by a pool, "Just standing like a tree with its roots reaching out to water." The vision, of course, is in the eye of the beholder: the old lady has ceased to be fearful because the living characters have ceased to be afraid of fear.

A similar ambiguity is suggested in two plays by James Reaney. Few women in Canadian literature have been used so uncompromisingly as symbols of evil pure and simple as Madam Fay, Muse of murders and suicides in *The Killdeer*, and Mrs. Charlotte Shade, abortionist and castrator in *The Sun and the Moon*. Yet it is less the principle of evil in the two women than the other characters' willingness to fear them and to accept their negative vision of life that does the harm. Although each provides the vital driving energy in her respective play – the "good" characters merely resist and respond – there is an air of insubstantiality about each, indicated by their names: Madam Fay, which sounds like a fortune-teller, with "Fay" suggesting "Fairy"; and Charlotte Shade, whose first name suggests "charlatan" and whose last suggests both darkness and incorporeality. Each is in fact a kind of fraudulent magician, conjuring up darkness and horrors which are dissipated and exposed by the forces of light. But neither character is defeated finally: both simply go away when the other characters will no longer play according to their scripts, to find, presumably, a more gullible audience. Madam Fay and Charlotte Shade are both Hecates pretending to be Venuses: they have control over death and hate, but they can control life and love only by destroying them. The latter control, however, depends on acquiescence in those whom they are subjugating. (In terms of the themes of *Survival*, this suggests that Reaney sees "inner awakening," the miraculous realization that you aren't a victim and perhaps have never really been one, as both necessary and sufficient for breaking the victim cycle. Reaney is unusual in that he typically jumps from Position Two to Position Four with no mention at all of Position Three.)

The positive "birth" and the negative "death" aspects of Nature are locked in combat in Joyce Marshall's short story, "The Old Woman." The plot is deceptively simple: Molly, an English war bride separated three years from her husband, joins him in Canada where he tends a remote power station in the North. She thinks the country will be picturesque but instead she finds it threatening; and her husband Toddy has changed, he has become withdrawn and strange. The isolation begins to tell on her but she finds an outside interest: she becomes unofficial midwife to the neighbouring French-Canadian families. Toddy resents and fears her absences from home. Before yet another excursion she walks to the powerhouse to let him know she's going and finds he's slipped over the edge into insanity: he is entirely hypnotized by the powerhouse machine.

At first this may appear to be a Nature versus Technology fight, with Molly, involved in "the miracle of new life" and saying things like "I brought a nice little boy into the world. He might never have been born except for me," representing the Birth-and-Love Goddess and the powerhouse, squat, grey and metallic, representing cold impersonal twentieth-century machinery, Henry Adams' Dynamo as Madonna. Certainly two female forces are struggling for possession of Toddy's soul, and the powerhouse – called by Toddy "the old woman," slang for wife – wins. "For years," says the assistant, "I watch him fall in love with her. Now she has him for herself." Union with the powerhouse is destructive and means insanity; but the powerhouse itself is less a representative of heavy industry than a condensed symbol of the landscape in which it is found. It is merely a converter of power, it does not produce it, and the power it converts is that of a waterfall. The noise of the waterfall and the all-encompassing snow, "blue and treacherous as steel," are the two aspects of the natural landscape Molly finds most threatening. Suggestive too is Toddy's fear of being "bushed" – going crazy from isolation in the North. In fact that *is* what happens to him; it is not the machines as such but the destructive power flowing through them that steals his soul. The Old Woman has done it again: Toddy closes himself off from human interaction, from life and birth, choosing instead an ugly marriage with the Snow Queen.

There are many more examples of powerful, negative old women in Canadian fiction: diseased old women, like the mother in Alice Munro's "The Peace of Utrecht," old ladies shut up in their sterile, life-denying houses, as in Anne Hébert's "The House on the Esplanade" and P. K. Page's "The Green Bird"; or, for fun (and treated somewhat more kindly by their

230

authors) the wizened spinster Marilla in *Anne of Green Gables* and the raucous, blood-sucking, vital old grandmother in *Jalna*.

The most extended portrait of the frozen old woman is presented by Margaret Laurence in *The Stone Angel*. The Angel itself is a statue in a cemetery, and the narrator and central character, Hagar Shipley, sees herself as a woman who has been in some way petrified all her life – petrified, in the dual sense of turned to stone and terrified. She too, like the old lady and Greta in *The Double Hook*, has tried to close life out, to impose on others, notably her husband and children, her own rectilineal sense of what should be allowed. At the beginning of the novel she is ninety years old and at its end she dies in a hospital, having reviewed her life and found it wanting. Hagar, tough, acerbic, self-critical and angry, takes the Canadian old-woman figure about as far towards being human as can be expected.

Like her namesake in the Bible, Hagar is an outcast in a wilderness. She is also the wilderness. What you are supposed to do with wildernesses, according to the Bible, is to somehow induce roses to blossom in them. Where have all the flowers gone? Away, usually. Venus makes few appearances in Canadian literature, and even for those she chooses odd incarnations.

Venus traditionally provides two things: sexual love and babies. There is a strange tendency in Canadian literature to split these functions apart, to have the sexual love department presided over by whores, or by easy and therefore despised women, and to reserve the babies for Diana figures, nonentities or even Hecates. This tendency is just as evident, if not more so, in the literature of French Canada as in that of the rest of the country. In Carrier's *La Guerre, Yes Sir!* Molly the prostitute is not even allowed to be French – she's an *anglaise*. Most of the other women are bloated wives (the one exception being Amélie, who has *two* men and is none too well thought of).

Jean Le Moyne notes this pattern in his essay "Women and French-Canadian Literature," and connects the dead young beloveds and unattractive "mature" women with the taboos set up by identifying "wife" always as "mother."

In English Canadian literature there are the pocket-picking prostitutes in *The Double Hook*, the whores in Callaghan's *Such Is My Beloved*, the older woman Bess who sleeps with everyone in *The Mountain and the Valley*, James Reaney's cannibalistic Whores of Babylon with their painted mouths (see especially "Rachel" in *One-Man Masque*). Something that looks like a real Venus figure makes an appearance in Callaghan's *The Loved and the Lost* – though even here, neither author nor central character can decide whether or not she's really a Virgin Mary – but her society can't tolerate her and she's murdered. In any case, Canadian literature is not strong on orgiastic sexuality and these figures are usually more conspicuous by their absence, by their two-dimensionality or by the curtains of silence drawn across their activities than by their presence in the foreground. They have neither the sexual attractiveness nor the power possessed by the bitch-goddesses in American literature, discussed by Leslie Fiedler in *Love and Death in the American Novel*; nor are they ever allowed the wise womanliness often characteristic of "mature" Venus-figures in European fiction. There's a suggestive poem by Alden Nowlan, "This Woman's Shaped For Love," which describes a creature that externally seems to be a perfect Venus; but the truth is revealed in the last two lines – she's actually another Ice Virgin:

And nights – her husband kneads in fists of rage
flesh that no human touch can animate.

Where, then, do babies come from? Usually out of thin air, with little to explain their genesis. The Great Canadian Baby is a literary institution; it could in some cases be termed the Baby Ex Machina, since it is lowered at the end of the book to solve problems for the characters which they obviously can't solve for themselves. The baby which terminates Sinclair Ross's *As For Me and My House*, for instance (if they think *that's* going to save their marriage they're crazy); and the one which provides a spiritual gaze for the defeated hero of John Marlyn's *Under the Ribs of Death*; and the one – though this one is more integrated with the symbolism of the book – that Lenchen has in the final pages of *The Double Hook*; and the saving baby at the end of *The Killdeer*; I throw in also the goose eggs that start the cycle anew after the Christmas slaughter of the geese in Reaney's *A Suit of Nettles*. Magic babies like this have a lot to do with the Canadian habit of predicting great things for the future (since the present is such a notable failure).

The women who produce these babies are more likely to be Dianas or Hecates than Venuses. Certainly Judith in *As For Me and My House*, with her narrow pinched white face, is hardly a cornucopia of unbridled sensuality; the seduction scene is conveyed by a single muted sound heard through a closed door, and Judith dies in childbirth anyway. (Dianas, in Canadian literature, have a way of dying: for instance, Effie in *The Mountain and the Valley* dies, a mere adolescent still.) Lenchen is a young girl, as Reaney's birth-giving females invariably are. And those are *good* babies, babies whose arrival signals spiritual rebirth for the other characters. There are also "bad" babies, like the endless series of infants that keep appearing like little piglets, born to nonentity mothers, in Marie-Claire Blais's *A Season in the Life of Emmanuel* and in the works of Frederick Philip Grove, most notably *Our Daily Bread*.

Cancer of the womb, exhausting miscarriages and deaths in childbirth abound. There are also those characters who try to produce babies and fail, like Mrs. Bentley in *As For Me and My House*, whose child is stillborn, like everything else she does; and the sterilized Margaret in MacLennan's *Each Man's Son*; and Rachel in Margaret Laurence's *A Jest of God*, who thinks she is pregnant but manages to squeeze out nothing more than a tumour, and a benign one at that (what an image of complete sterility; a malignant one would at least have been *growing*). The Great Canadian Baby is sometimes alarmingly close to the Great Canadian Coffin (a whole book could be written exploring the coffin-funeral syndrome in Canadian literature), and for the magic levitation of cradle out of coffin, see James Reaney's *One-Man Masque*. But stunted or doomed fertility, the identity of birth and death, are what might be expected from the Ice Goddess. Given this state of affairs, it is little wonder that the central figure in Graeme Gibson's *Communion* prefers making love to two stone statues in a cemetery – Stone Angels again – rather than to any real women.

The connections between landscape and culture and the kinds of female figures that can be expected from them are fully drawn in the Lucan section of Gibson's *Five Legs*. The real Venus is missing: she has departed for Europe, pregnant and taking with her whatever fecundity Lucan's life ever contained, having refused his demand that she get an abortion. His present wife cannot conceive. He fixes on an apparent Diana, knowing, good Canadian as he is, that Dianas are the proper source of children; but this Diana, whose name in the book is Susan, is really a destructive Hecate in disguise, a cold repressive old woman masquerading as a young girl. Like the embrace of the giant ice virgins, union with her will mean death; she's already polished off the inhabitant of the Great Canadian Coffin at the centre of the book, who did little more than propose to her (there was little more he *could* do, since she's a frigid virgin). Susan wants her men to conform to the culture she represents, the culture of potential denied. The landscape is covered with snow. The time is winter.

Are there any real women? Or rather, are there any women in Canadian literature who appear to be leading normal married lives, having children who are not dead, or Gothic morons like Patrice in Blais's *Mad Shadows*, or so numerous they don't matter? Well . . . Minn in Marian Engel's *The Honeyman Festival*. Stacey in Margaret Laurence's *The Fire Dwellers*. But neither seems to be enjoying life much, their children are a drain or a worry, their husbands are hostile, incommunicative or not there.

This topic leads into the Rapunzel Syndrome, which seems to be a pattern – not just a Canadian pattern – for "realistic" novels about "normal" women. In the Rapunzel Syndrome there are four elements: Rapunzel, the main character; the wicked witch who has imprisoned her, usually her mother or her husband, sometimes her father or grandfather; the tower she's imprisoned in – the attitudes of society, symbolized usually by her house and children which society says she must not abandon; and the Rescuer, a handsome prince of little substantiality who provides momentary escape. In the original Rapunzel story the Rescuer is a solution and the wicked witch is vanquished; in the Rapunzel Syndrome the Rescuer is not much help. In *The Honeyman Festival* he is only a memory of a dead film director; in *The Fire Dwellers* he's an unbelievable much younger man who writes science fiction; in *A Jest of God*, which also displays the Rapunzel Syndrome, he's a visiting trifler, and a married one at that. The Rescuer's facelessness and lack of substance as a character is usually a clue to his status as a fantasy-escape figure; Rapunzel is in fact stuck in the tower, and the best thing she can do is learn how to cope with it.

The Rapunzel Syndrome transcends national boundaries. What is Canadian about the local exemplars of the Rapunzel figure is their difficulty in communicating, or even acknowledging, their fears and hatreds; they walk around with mouths like clenched fists. If they fit any of Graves's categories, they are probably women who would rather be Dianas or Venuses but find themselves trapped against their will inside Hecates. In fact, in Canada *Rapunzel and the tower are the same.* These heroines have internalized the values of their culture to such an extent that they have become their own prisons. The *real* struggle in *The Fire Dwellers* and in *The Honeyman Festival* is the struggle of the Diana, capable of freedom, and of the "good" Venus, capable of love both maternal and sexual, to find a way out of the rigid Hecate stereotype in which she finds herself shut like a moth in a chrysalis. This struggle is taking place also in *The Stone Angel,* and Hagar's two "free" acts that she can remember – tiny though they are – strike the reader as triumphant, simply because they are measured against so overwhelmingly negative and limiting a pattern. This is true also of Minn's instinctive attack on the policeman in *The Honeyman Festival;* it may not be much, but in view of Minn's hatreds and despairs it is at least a flicker of life.

It's interesting that all these women – Stacey, Hagar, Minn – visualize their imprisonment by thinking of themselves as trapped in bodies which they do not recognize as theirs: Stacey's distorted by fat, Minn's by pregnancy, Hagar's by old age. The same pattern – the loving, potentially beautiful woman trapped inside a negative shell – is present in Ross's Mrs. Bentley, who is only thirty-four but who looks and often talks and thinks like a much older woman. The process itself – the takeover by the Hecate stereotype, despite the character's efforts to evade it – may be observed in the character Margaret in David Helwig's novel *The Day Before Tomorrow*, with her dead child, her obsessions with God and Death and her pathetically dwindling attempts to participate in life despite the role she's trapped in. At its most desperate and grotesque, the pattern produces characters like the diseased mother in Munro's "The Peace of Utrecht"; the "real" mother continues to exist inside her deteriorating body, gradually cut off from communication, her last meaningful act a (failed) escape from the hospital where she's been imprisoned.

Perhaps this pattern gives us a clue to the full shape of the Nature-Woman metaphor in Canadian literature: not just an Ice-Virgin-Hecate figure, but a Hecate with Venus and Diana trapped inside. And perhaps the "plots" – the stories that can be told – about the Ice-Virgin-Hecate Nature-Monster are not limited to how one is destroyed by or manages to escape or conquer this figure; the story can also be about the attempts of the buried Venuses and Dianas to get out, to free themselves. This is suggested by Jay Macpherson's poem "The Caverned Woman," which opens this chapter. In it there is a Woman-as-Land figure, or perhaps it is Land-as-Woman; the metaphor is evenly balanced. On the outside this giantess seems to be a Hecate-Ice-Goddess of the kind we have been discussing: cold, "Ice-bound," hard. But seen from within the figure is a Venus, filled with the "Seraph forms" of inspiration, with "flowers and fountains," the fertility of the natural world, and with the "milk and blood" of human fecundity and birth. Venus is not necessarily absent but concealed.

Short List:

ENGEL, Marian, *The Honeyman Festival*; AN, $2.50.
LAURENCE, Margaret, *The Fire Dwellers*; NCL, $2.50.

LAURENCE, Margaret, *The Stone Angel*; NCL, $2.50.

WATSON, Sheila, *The Double Hook*; NCL, $1.50.

Long List:

BIRNEY, Earle, "The Mammoth Corridors," *Rag & Bone Shop*; M&S.

BLAIS, Marie-Claire, *A Season in the Life of Emmanuel*; Grossets Universal Library.

BLAIS, Marie-Claire, *Mad Shadows*; NCL.

BUCKLER, Ernest, *The Mountain and the Valley*; NCL.

CARRIER, Roch, *La Guerre, Yes Sir!*; AN.

ENGEL, Marian, *The Honeyman Festival*; AN.

FIEDLER, Leslie, *Love and Death in the American Novel*; Meridian.

GIBSON, Graeme, *Communion*; AN.

GIBSON, Graeme, *Five Legs*; AN.

GROVE, Frederick Philip, *Our Daily Bread*; OP.

GRAVES, Robert, *The White Goddess*; Faber.

HÉBERT, Anne, "The House on the Esplanade," W1.

HELWIG, David, *The Day Before Tomorrow*; Oberon.

LAURENCE, Margaret, *A Jest of God*; M&S. Or, *Rachel, Rachel*; Popular Library.

LAURENCE, Margaret, *The Fire Dwellers*; NCL.

LAURENCE, Margaret, *The Stone Angel*; NCL.

Le MOYNE, Jean, "Women and French-Canadian Literature," in *Convergences* (trans. Philip Stratford); R.

MacEWEN, Gwen, *Terror and Erebus*; C.B.C. play (not in print).

MacLENNAN, Hugh, *Each Man's Son*; Macmillan.

MacPHERSON, Jay, "The Caverned Woman," *The Boatman*; OUP.

MARLYN, John, *Under the Ribs of Death*; NCL.

MARSHALL, Joyce, "The Old Woman", W1.

MONTGOMERY, L. M., *Anne of Green Gables*; McGraw.

MUNRO, Alice, "The Peace of Utrecht", W2.

NOWLAN, Alden, "This Woman Shaped for Love," *Under the Ice*; R, OP.

PAGE, P. K., "The Green Bird"; W1.

PRATT, E. J., *Towards the Last Spike*; Macmillan. Also *Selected Poems*; Macmillan.

REANEY, James, *A Suit of Nettles*; Macmillan.

REANEY, James, *One-Man Masque*; *The Killdeer and Other Plays*; Macmillan. "Rachel" also in PMC.

REANEY, James, "The Canadian Poet's Predicament" in *Masks of Poetry* (ed. A.J.M. Smith); NCL.

REANEY, James, *The Killdeer*; *The Killdeer and Other Plays*; Macmillan.

REANEY, James, *The Sun and the Moon*; *The Killdeer and Other Plays*; Macmillan.

De La ROCHE, Mazo, *Jalna*; Macmillan.

ROSS, Sinclair, *As For Me and My House*; NCL.

WATSON, Sheila, *The Double Hook*; NCL.

WILSON, Ethel, *Swamp Angel*; Macmillan.

11

QUÉBEC: BURNING MANSIONS

She had a sense of being imprisoned within these four walls
only to suffer, and for nothing else.

> – *Gabrielle Roy,*
> The Tin Flute

My children you dance badly
One must admit it is difficult to dance here
In this lack of air
Here without any space which is the whole of the dance.

> – *Saint-Denys-Garneau,*
> "Spectacle of the Dance"

An entire lifetime had taught them that they could do nothing.

> – *Roch Carrier,*
> La Guerre, Yes Sir!

I live in a land where cold has conquered
green things, reigns grey and heavy over phantom
trees.

I am a silent part of a race that shivers in its
sleep under frost-bound words, whose frail quick
speech is fading.

I am part of a cry all around me
stone with no language
steep cliff
bare blade in my winter heart

> – *Yves Préfontaine,*
> "Country to Let"

My mission is suicide, everywhere and forever. A whole nation crouches within me, retelling its lost childhood in bursts of stammering words and delirious pages, and, under the dark shock of lucidity, suddenly weeping before the immensity of the disaster and the almost-sublime dimensions of its failure. There comes a time, after two centuries of conquest and thirty-four years of sadness, when one no longer has the strength to push beyond this terrible vision.

– Hubert Aquin,
Prochain Episode

In my dreams there is no longer anything hanging on the trees but rotten fruit, and I don't see flowers any more. It's winter everywhere. It's cold. But the saddest part, really, is to have lost my appetite.

– Marie-Claire Blais,
A Season in the Life of Emmanuel

I approach this chapter with some trepidation, since I'm far from being well-read in Québec literature. Although I've done some of my reading in the original (usually with the aid of a dictionary, I must confess), I've relied for the most part on translations, which can narrow your range considerably. For instance, if I were French-speaking and wanted to read English Canadian literature through translations, I'd be confined at the moment to fewer than ten novels. Though the situation is better for the English-Canadian wishing to explore Québec, and improving all the time, there are still a lot of books which should be available and aren't. However, I'm assuming you're like me – that is, you learned French in high school, you can blurt out a few phrases when necessary, and you can read it but not fluently. Therefore I've limited the discussion in this chapter to works available in translation.

If you're a French teacher teaching Canadian literature, presumably you already know more about this area than I do; for you, there ought to be a book written in French, describing more of the key patterns in Québec literature, and with a single chapter on "English" Canada parallel to this one.

What, then, is a visitor to French Canadian literature apt to find? What are the similarities and the differences? I'll make a couple of general observations and then proceed to individual works.

Like a tourist, I noticed surface differences first. Québec literature, like that of English Canada, abounds in religious imagery; but whereas the rest of Canada goes in more for Old Testament and Biblical imagery, and especially for heroes such as David and Noah, Québec literature, naturally enough, prefers liturgical images; saints, martyrs, sacramental objects and Christ loom large. Nevertheless, both "halves" tend to choose the negative rather than the positive versions of the religious symbolisms made available to them by their respective cultures. That is, English Canada depicts failed Davids rather than triumphant ones, Noahs that sink more often than they float; it chooses Moses wandering in the wilderness rather than Joshua entering the Promised Land. And French Canada prefers saints and martyrs at the moment of their suffering, mutilation or death to the same figures received in glory, and Christ on the cross to Christ in any other version (Divine Babe, Resurrected Saviour, teacher and healer, and so forth).

That was a difference concealing a similarity; now here's a similarity concealing a difference. Québec authors have been just as addicted to Survivalism as have those in the rest of Canada. But the attitude and its corollaries have been with them longer, and are, if anything, more extreme. In addition to the bare survivalism they share with the rest of Canada – survival in the face of a harsh climate and a recalcitrant land – and the sense that their survival may be the survival of an archaic form of life, which they also share – they emphasize cultural and religious survivalism. French Canada must cling to its language-and-religion life-raft in the sea of hostile English Protestants which threatens to engulf it. Because the social group is more cohesive, the walls of the garrison can be erected higher and stronger than anywhere else in Canada, with a corresponding intensification of the feelings of suffocation inside the garrison and terror of what lies outside.

A good place to start when you're looking at the wall, its effects, and what goes on inside it is of course Louis Hémon's *Maria Chapdelaine*. I won't say much about this book, as I assume it's well-known; but I will indicate that the marital choices open to Maria are significant. Each of the men represents a way of life: one offers escape to the United States; one a repetition of the static farm life – hard work and child-bearing – that has exhausted Maria's mother; the third might have combined dynamic growth with continuity of cultural values, but Nature the Monster kills him in the forest. Maria finally chooses to remain, marry the second, and become an incarnation of her mother; and a chorus of earth-spirit, ancestral and heavenly voices backs her up. The bleak and confined life inside the wall is preferable to the threatening emptiness that lies outside it.

Ringuet's *Thirty Acres* picks up this theme. In it, the protagonist wants to make Maria's choice – dedication to the old ways and the land – but somehow the old ways and the land betray him. He loses his beloved farm and is forced to move to the United States; which, far from being a Promised Land, is a scene of exile and desolation. His son, who has taken over the farm, can't make it work very well either. The final picture of the father, Euchariste Moisan, is that of a defeated old man, working as a watchman in a garage filled with the machines he hates, wondering why he has failed, or why the land has failed him. "So that's how things were," he thinks; "even the land no longer supported her children." Neither staying with the land nor leaving it provides much beyond bare survival.

Maria Chapdelaine and *Thirty Acres* can be read as a kind of background to the increasingly more desperate fictions which follow them. Maria's world offers her security, though at the price of her individuality. Old man Moisan, marooned in the city though he is, cherishes the rural world he has lost, and has at least the security of his own unshaken opinions. Both are firmly rooted in the family and in tradition. But as the two poles of Québec experience – static life on the farm and rootlessness in the city – become further and further separated from each other, in time as well as in lifestyle, they are reflected with increasing intensity by Québec authors: the farm becomes a claustrophobic nightmare, crawling with lice and babies, spawning brutality and despair; the city becomes a mechanical void, through which the individual who has managed to escape his family wanders lost and helpless.

A novel which catches this development halfway between oppressive security and freefloating hysteria – or between the last gasp of Position Two and the beginning of Position Three, if you like – is Gabrielle Roy's *The Tin Flute*. It depicts a marriage between a latter-day Maria Chapdelaine and a Euchariste Moisan who fails earlier in life. Rose-Anna has all Maria's resignation and long-suffering patience, but it doesn't get her anywhere; her husband Azarius can't handle the city any better than could Moisan. The family that results drifts from slum-house to slum-house, trapped in poverty, spawning fresh babies at every turn, and suffering two events that we come to recognize as archetypal Québec literary occurrences: the death of a young child (from leukemia, which the doctor calls "a disease of apathy"), and the decision of a daughter to become a nun. Though Roy's approach is milder, more detached and less acerbic than that of the writers who follow her into this territory, death and renunciation seem logical responses to the life that awaits the children in this hopeless world. Azarius solves his problem by joining the army, which will assure Rose-Anna a monthly cheque, but which for him is virtual suicide.

Two novels by the same author which deal separately with these poles – what happens in the rural village, what happens in the city – are Roch Carrier's *La Guerre, Yes Sir!* and *Is It the Sun, Philibert?* In the first, two men return to their village from the War. One is in a coffin, the other on temporary leave. The world of the village is coarse enough, but it has a certain social cohesiveness; the outside world of the War has the brutality without the safety, and in it the French Canadian, who though he may have been known as a ne'er-do-well in his own village was at least well-known, finds himself a non-person. The real conflict from the point of view of the villagers is between themselves and the *Anglais*, represented by the soldiers who accompany the coffin (these are actual Englishmen, not English Canadians; often in Québec literature little distinction is made between the two).

The battle royal, the only physical and visible "war" in the book, is between the villagers and the soldiers, whom they sense as their oppressors, fought for the territory of the coffin. Much attention is paid by Carrier to the chain of oppressors and victims: the soldier Bérubé has been brutalized by the *Anglais* army, where his job is cleaning toilets. Instead of directing his anger against the Army, however, he spends a considerable amount of time beating up the hog-butcher Arsène, passing on his own sufferings in a parody of army procedure:

> "Arsène, I'm going to make a good soldier out of you. Tell me exactly what you see when you look in the mirror."
>
> "I see myself."
>
> Bérubé brought back his fist to make him understand that the threat was stronger. "One last time. What do you see in the mirror?"
>
> "I see a pile of shit."
>
> Bérubé had won. He smiled; he hugged Arsène. He patted his cheek. "Now you're a real good soldier."

But Arsène had earlier been observed dealing out the same kind of treatment to his son Philibert: the victim-victimizer chain, it seems, is complex and endless. Again, neither the outside world of war and the *Anglais* nor the enclosed, tightly-knit, static world of the village seems a viable setting for a free and enjoyable human life.

In *Is It the Sun, Philibert?* Carrier reverses the movement of the protagonist who this time leaves the village instead of returning to it. Philibert, son of the hog-butcher Arsène, runs away as soon as he can escape the violence and brutality of his father. The first part of the book is a series of short vignettes of village life as experienced by the child, and each scene is either frightening or revolting. On the first page the father destroys Philibert's Christmas present in a particularly sadistic manner; his next memory is of a flock of ducks that get frozen in the ice and of the hunter who chops off their heads; his next is of the sounds of his parents' lovemaking, of the bed which creaks, "a tortured beast in the night"; and his next, of digging a miniature grave. (His father, as well as being a pig-killer, is also a grave-digger, making him a double death symbol.) Philibert can't lift the child's coffin he wishes to bury, so he inters his sister's doll instead: "Philibert was happy. It was just like a real funeral." Philibert, in fact, is a little death-baby, doomed from infancy. His main childhood resentment is that he isn't a spineless cripple like the twenty-one Laliberté children who are taken every year to the Church in a wheelbarrow procession so their parents can thank God for sending all of them. So we aren't surprised by the disasters of his life in Montréal, the nadir of which is his job in a boot factory during which he has a dream about *being* a boot.

It looks for a while as though Philibert is going to make it. He becomes the manager of a professional victim, "The Man With The Face of Steel," a giant who makes his living by letting people smash him in the face. The giant is tremendously popular: there are many who covet the chance to hit back, the only chance they will ever get. But the crowd goes overboard one day and the professional victim commits an action for which he cannot forgive himself: he strikes back. Overcome with remorse, he rows out into a lake and drowns himself.

But he leaves Philibert a fortune, which the latter decides to use to open a little grocery store (thus moving a step up the ladder, from worker to petty bourgeoisie . . .). On his way to collect, however, he wrecks his car on a roadside Cross of Christ. The last message the universe gives him comes from one of his own dying hallucinations: "You are suffering . . . you have always wanted to suffer."

Both of Carrier's books, but especially *Philibert*, raise a question which is central to Québec literature, and indeed to Canadian literature as a whole. Roughly stated, the question is: Who is responsible? We can see that Bérubé is a victim, we can see that Philibert's life is, as Sheila Fischman says in her Introduction, "a series of putdowns and failures." And in *Philibert*, the author is certainly pointing an accusing finger at the System, with the villain being both the English Canadians who are exploiting the French and the capitalists who are exploiting the workers (these two tend to be equated, needless to say). But the fact remains that it is not the System that wrecks Philibert's car: it is he himself. His role as victim is certainly imposed on him by the System, but it has also been imposed on him by his family and his culture, and he has internalized it very early. The repressiveness and brutality of his father and the impersonal oppressiveness of his life in Montréal reinforce each other. If you read the book simply as an attempt to pin the tail on the capitalist donkey, it doesn't work; Philibert's final disaster has much more complex causes, one of which is his acquiescence in his own suffering.

A joint symptom and cause of Philibert's unhappy end is his interest in death. His interest amounts in fact to an obsession, and in this Philibert is typical of the literature in which he appears. We've noted the general Canadian predilection for coffins, but in Québec this interest is intensified almost to a mania. Leslie Fiedler, in *Love and Death in the American Novel*, puts forward the thesis that in Europe the typical "initiation" for a young boy is his first encounter with sex, and in America it's his first encounter with killing (usually an animal). If the central European experience is sex and the central mystery "what goes on in the bedroom," and if the central American experience is killing and the central mystery is "what goes on in the forest" (or in the slum streets), surely the central Canadian experience is death and the central mystery is "what goes on in the coffin." Nowhere is this more evident than in Québec literature. I can think of three major examples without even trying. In *La Guerre, Yes Sir!* the character who occasions the action is a dead man in a coffin and the most important dream or fantasy is of an enormous coffin which is devouring the entire world:

> . . . the people from the village were entering it, one by one . . . just as they entered church, bent over, submissive. . . . Now people were arriving in crowds, whole villages at a time, huge numbers of people patiently awaiting their turn. . . . From the four corners of the earth people came running up, rushing into Corriveau's coffin which was swelling up like a stomach. . . . The entire ocean had been drunk up and in the whole world nothing remained but Corriveau's coffin.

Gérard Bessette's novel *Le Cycle* takes place entirely at a funeral; and in the brilliant film *Mon Oncle Antoine* (brilliant because it manages to fuse a number of central images and also to use the often too-slow NFB techniques while avoiding the usual static effects), the last shot is of the young protagonist with his nose pressed against the window, staring, not at the archetypal couple making love, but at the archetypal coffin *with the lid off*. This is the knowledge that is important, the film implies: not your first woman or your first murder but your first dead person.

An almost standard Québec vision of death is the vision of the dead baby (or dead babies); it's a fantasy often indulged in by mothers or grandmothers, and it's hard to tell whether they are torturing themselves with it or enjoying it, or both. Rose-Anna has this vision in *The Tin Flute*, at the moment when she is about to give birth yet again:

> . . . She saw Azarius carrying a little white coffin, very short and narrow, a tiny coffin. . . . Funerals, christenings, all the important events of life took on the same bitter, unfathomable character in her mind. Sometimes she perceived a freshly dug grave, all ready to receive the tiny coffin, and sometimes a sleeping infant in its christening dress. . . .

Grand-mère Antoinette in Blais's *A Season in the Life of Emmanuel* indulges in similar thoughts, though with more satisfaction:

> . . . There had been so many funerals during the years . . . so many little black corpses, in the wintertime, children always disappearing, babies who had lived only a few months. . . . Grand-mère Antoinette allowed herself to be rocked gently in the swell of all those deaths, suddenly submerged in a great and singular feeling of content. . . .

It's therefore right on target when, in her story "Bernadette," the English Canadian writer Mavis Gallant ends her story about a pregnant French Canadian servant girl with an almost identical vision:

. . . It would be born, and it would die. That it would die she never doubted. She was uncertain of so much else; her own body was a mystery, nothing had ever been explained. . . . She saw, as plainly as if it had been laid in her arms, her child, her personal angel, white and swaddled, baptized, ready for death.

Birth as death, the Infant Saviour as corpse. Though the story is "about" Québec rather than "by" Québec, it catches the mood perfectly.

This obsession with death is not very cheering, but neither is it precisely morbid; it is simply an image which reflects a state of soul. What the image says is that the Québec situation (or the Canadian situation) is dead or death-dealing, and therefore genuine knowledge of it must be knowledge of death. It is also an image of ultimate sterility and powerlessness, the final result of being a victim. Images of dead people in their coffins translate readily into images of oneself dead in one's own coffin, and Québec poets have a disconcerting way of imagining themselves as dead. In "The Closed Room," Anne Hébert has a vision of herself martyred, with heart removed:

> The bright colour of blood
> Seals the hollow vault
> And my hands folded
> Over this devastated space
> Grow cold and fascinated with emptiness.

In another poem, "There is Certainly Someone," she begins abruptly, "There is certainly someone / Who once killed me. . . ." "But I am a dead girl," Michèle Lalonde says in "Le

Jour Halluciné," without surprise. Saint-Denys-Garneau's poems are thronged with such images. Heart as bird as death, for instance, in "Bird Cage":

> I am a bird cage
> A cage of bone
> With a bird
>
> The bird in the cage of bone
> Is death building his nest. . . .

———◆———

A book which bears the same relation to these themes – the acquiescence in one's role as victim, the obsession with death – that, for instance, Cohen's *Beautiful Losers* does to Indians-as-victims and Gibson's *Communion* does to animals-as-victims is Marie-Claire Blais's *A Season in the Life of Emmanuel*. Again we find the poverty-stricken rural family, the mother drained by too-numerous babies, the coarse male figures who brutalize those weaker than themselves, the dying child, the daughter who elects to escape by becoming a nun. But the *willing* participation of the characters in the perpetuation of their own misery is here rendered explicitly. The two young boys, Number Seven, destined to become a criminal, and Jean-Le Maigre, slated for death, are enormously interested both in their own sufferings and in those of others:

> "I once knew a man who was very ill," said Number Seven (he didn't dare admit that he had greatly enjoyed Grand-père Napoleon's death agony), "iller than you are, he used to cough and spit blood." ("But I spit blood too,"

Jean-Le Maigre put in, offended that anyone should show
a lack of respect toward an illness he loved like a sister.)

They accumulate beatings like merit badges, and amuse
themselves by hearing each others' confessions of sins, real
or imagined, for which they dream up visions of painful punishment. Wallowing in misery is a family pastime. One older
brother has committed suicide, the drained and obliterated
mother wanders about the house at night sorrowing for dead
babies whose names she can't even remember correctly, the
sister Héloise stays in her room, fasting and torturing herself
with masochistic sexual-religious fantasies. The world beyond
the family merely extends its preoccupations. The two boys
first experience life on the outside through a degrading Reform
School whose Director loves inflicting punishment. In the seminary where Jean-Le Maigre is later sent to die, the boys are
entertained at meals with stories of saints being tortured, which
they enjoy immensely. It's no surprise that the Brother in charge
of the infirmary has been quietly hastening the deaths of his
little charges because death turns him on; nor that his secret
desire is to be beaten with his own belt. In such a world, pain
is almost the only strong sensation available, and the characters
take what pleasure they can from it. When Héloise exchanges
her convent and her family for a whorehouse, it isn't just a
change from two authoritarian matriarchal institutions to a
third: it's also a change from one kind of mortification of the
flesh to another. And the author doesn't victimize her characters; she observes – through a nightmarish lens, to be sure
– how they victimize themselves.

The Emmanuel of the title is the family's latest baby, but
though he is named after the Redeemer it's obvious he won't
redeem anything. On the day of his birth he begins absorbing
the lessons of his culture: ". . . it seemed to him suddenly that

he had already been familiar for a long while with cold, with hunger, and perhaps even with despair." And later in the book, he's learning – at his grandmother's knee – to enjoy catastrophe. As she recites her litanies of disaster, the baby Emmanuel listens entranced:

> . . . But he was very fond of bad news, as a matter of fact. Like his brothers, he was to love gales and hurricanes, shipwrecks and funerals, when he grew up. . . .

Two other themes which haunt Québec literature are focussed here also: the theme of thwarted incest (in a literature so family-centred, there are few other available love-objects) and the theme of total entrapment. The plight of English Canadian characters trapped by their family ties seems mild compared with that of the French Canadian ones: in Québec, it seems, you can't leave home *at all*, and if you do you'll want to go back, no matter how miserable home was when you actually lived there. Jean-Le Maigre, dying in the infirmary, has an hallucination in which he's trying to escape from the seminary in order to return home. His hallucination ends in death, and in fact many escaped characters, when they or even their thoughts turn homewards, suffer a similar fate: Philibert, for instance, has been thinking of going home just before his fatal car crash. In the Québec novel, the family is a claustrophobic inferno, but freeing yourself from it emotionally and returning to it once you've technically made your getaway are equally impossible. No wonder coffins seem preferable.

It's interesting that Jean-Le Maigre is a writer, and a precocious and talented one. The problem for his English Canadian counterparts is that they can't seem to write, though no one is visibly prohibiting them. Jean-Le Maigre is prolific enough – he pours out morbid little poems, and equally death-oriented prose musings. But at home his father and grandmother destroy his works, and by the time he reaches the infirmary he's dying anyway. He is impeded more by external circumstances – other people and disease – than he is by psychological blockage. This is true of another writer in a different novel, Hubert Aquin's *Prochain Episode*. Here the writer is literally imprisoned; he's in an institution for the criminally insane, and everything he writes (and he too is prolific) is presumably snatched from him to be treated as "evidence" by lawyers and psychiatrists. Jean-Le Maigre's disease and confinement and Aquin's nameless hero's imprisonment and sense of futility as a writer are symptoms of malaise which may be compared with the English Canadian counterparts discussed in Chapter Nine. The French Canadian artist has an advantage in that he can actually get the words down on paper, with whatever difficulty. His problem is getting the paper, the message, into the larger world before it is destroyed.

Philibert has acquiesced in his role as victim, Jean-Le Maigre has embraced his joyfully; Aquin's hero tries to reject his, and his attempts to do so are revealing indeed. *Prochain Episode* is a semi-allegorical treatment of the plight of Québec. The hero is a Separatist spy and guerilla operating in Europe; his mistress is the beautiful K, with whom he is never tired of equating his beautiful country Kébec. K sets him a task: he is to kill an elusive enemy with a multiple identity, who has the power to sabotage the revolutionaries' plans for freeing Québec by force of arms. He tracks down his intended victim, but when he has captured him and is about to squeeze the trigger, his enemy mesmerizes him by a double ruse: he claims to be someone else, thus filling the hero with self-doubt; and he tells a sob-story in which he himself features as the victim, thus paralyzing the hero with pity. (It is of interest that the story he repeats is almost a duplicate of the fabricated story the hero has earlier told *him*: both are lying, and both are using the traditional Canadian themes of failure and misery as a weapon. The fascinating thing is that in both cases the weapon works.) The hero and his enemy – who may represent English Canada – are reflections of each other; and it's even suggested that the beautiful K may be dallying with both of them at the same time.

In any case, the hero's failure to act, to kill or even definitely identify his enemy, costs him his freedom. The enemy escapes, and the hero loses K and returns to Montréal where he is betrayed into the hands of the authorities by parties unknown. His revolution, his rejection of his role as victim, has collapsed because at the crucial moment he was suckered in by someone else playing that very role. In prison he speculates both about the reasons for his failure and about the future. The next time, he thinks, it won't end the same way: he'll kill his enemy, reunite himself with his beloved, and the revolution will succeed. The revolution itself is visualized as a destructive but purgative bloodbath or Armageddon, to be followed by a rather indistinct but pleasurable future. Which leads us to another motif in Québec literature, the Incendiary or Burning Mansion theme.

English Canadian literature is not overly-disposed towards fires, but Québec authors love having their characters start them or die in them. The two boys in *A Season in the Life of Emmanuel* are sent to Reform School for burning down their schoolhouse, Philibert ends his life in a burst of flame, a whole congregation fries in Carrier's *Floralie, Where Are You?* and Aquin's hero, though not actually a firebug, would like nothing better than to shoot up the tasteful but empty chateau inhabited by his enemy. Part of this preference for fire may stem from religious tradition: fire as a purgatorial burning-away of disease or sin. But this theme is also connected with the Ancestral

House motif. The ancestral house – the "manor" in Anne Hébert's poem "Manor Life," which is empty and stifling and can provide only imitations of love, the furniture-crammed and threatening chateau in Aquin's novel, Philibert's grandparents' house which has been sold to strangers and is full of pigs – all these represent Québec tradition, or history in general, in various stages of stagnation or decay. And since the "house" – the tradition – is also a trap, burning it down is viewed by some as a delightful temptation.

This combination – purgative fire plus ancestral house – is present undiluted in Jacques Ferron's story "Cadieu." Here the house is an old one, "dating from the time of the Indians," an "ancestral home," the property of Cadieu's father. By the time Cadieu is born the house is in a state of "destitution." Cadieu himself is the oldest of "five, seven, ten" children: they seem to increase geometrically. As soon as Cadieu grows up he leaves the village. On the way he encounters a weird beggar with magic powers connected with birth, who asks him how many children he wants. He says (remembering no doubt his crowded home) that he doesn't want any; almost immediately he gets VD and, overcome with shame, changes his name. Eventually he becomes a successful businessman, still using his alias:

After five or six years a successful man was I – gloves, hat, the lot. I even had friends in the government. But I still bore the name I had taken in shame. To that of my forebears I longed to return, longed to replant the family tree, to have an umbrella of ancestral skin with micro-filmed tattoos, bleeding heart and fleur de lys.

He goes back to his family village, but his father doesn't recognize him. He buys the ancestral house and sets fire to it "in order to free it." During the blaze the prophetic beggar reappears, and comments, "What a good fire!"

Burning down a house in order to free it is a motif found not only in Québec: Sheila Watson uses it in *The Double Hook*, but that book ends with a birth. Cadieu, however, will never replant the family tree: the beggar or his disease has deprived him of that ability. The fire that consumes his house is final, but it is an ambiguous fire. Perhaps, as the beggar says, it is a good fire. The longing for the shelter of an "umbrella of ancestral skin," with its suggestion of Hitler lampshades and its masochistic tattoos, is possibly not one that should be indulged. But the horns of the dilemma are severe – a return to the ancestral ways of the victimized, or the destruction of everything.

The drastic nature of Cadieu's solution dramatizes the drastic nature of his problem; it also dramatizes the difficulty of directing constructive anger towards a real external enemy (he burns down his *own* house) and the difficulty of envisaging a future beyond the conflagration.

In many ways, Québec's situation – as reflected in its literature – epitomizes the situation of Canada as a whole; but whereas Québec authors may have trouble imagining the world after the fire, English Canadian ones are just beginning to imagine the fire itself.

Short List:

AQUIN, Hubert, *Prochain Episode*; NCL, $1.95 (translated by Penny Williams).

BLAIS, Marie-Claire, *A Season in the Life of Emmanuel*; Grosset's Universal Library, $2.50 (translated by Derek Coltman).

CARRIER, Roch, *La Guerre, Yes Sir!*; AN, $2.50 (translated by Sheila Fischman).

GLASSCO, John, ed., *The Poetry of French Canada in Translation*; OUP, $4.00.

ROY, Gabrielle, *The Tin Flute*; NCL, $1.95 (translated by Hannah Josephson).

Long List:

AQUIN, Hubert, *Prochain Episode*; NCL.

BESSETTE, Gérard, *Le Cycle*; Editions du Jour; (not yet in translation).

BLAIS, Marie-Claire, *A Season in the Life of Emmanuel*; Grosset's Universal Library.

CARRIER, Roch, *Floralie, Where Are You?*; AN.

CARRIER, Roch, *Is It the Sun, Philibert?*; AN.

CARRIER, Roch, *La Guerre, Yes Sir!*; AN.

COHEN, Leonard, *Beautiful Losers*; Bantam.

FERRON, Jacques, "Cadieu," *Tales from the Uncertain Country*; AN.

GALLANT, Mavis, "Bernadette", W2.

GIBSON, Graeme, *Communion*; AN.

HÉBERT, Anne, "Manor Life" (trans. F. R. Scott).

HÉBERT, Anne, "The Closed Room" (trans. F. R. Scott).

HÉMON, Louis, *Maria Chapdelaine*; Macmillan.

LaLONDE, Michèle, "Le Jour Halluciné" (trans. A.J.M. Smith).

RINGUET, *Thirty Acres*; NCL.

ROY, Gabrielle, *The Tin Flute*; NCL.

SAINT-DENYS-GARNEAU, "Bird Cage" (trans. F. R. Scott).

All poems quoted are from *The Poetry of French Canada in Translation* (ed. John Glassco); OUP.

For more comparative insights on French Canadian literature, see *Butterfly on Rock* and *Second Image* (both listed under Other Books of Criticism); and the magazine *Ellipse*, available through C.P. 10, Faculté des Arts, Université de Sherbrooke, Sherbrooke, Québec.

12

JAIL-BREAKS AND RE-CREATIONS

What are you . . . ? they ask.
And she replies: I am the wind that wants a flag.
I am the mirror of your picture
until you make me the marvel of your life.
Yes, I am one and none, pin and pine, snow and slow,
America's attic, an empty room,
a something possible, a chance, a dance
that is not danced. A cold kingdom.
. . . .
What is the matter then . . . ? they ask, and some are
                                                   indifferent,
What is the matter then . . . ? they ask.
. . . .
The matter is the promise that was never taken. . . .

> – *Patrick Anderson,*
> "Poem on Canada"

For we are a conquered nation: sea to sea we bartered
everything that counts, till we have
nothing to lose but our forebears' will to lose.
Beautiful riddance!
And some will make their choice and eat imperial meat.
But many will come to themselves, for there is
no third way at last. . . .

> – *Dennis Lee,*
> Civil Elegies

Consider the Poles. They have built a nation which, if not great and powerful, is at least distinct.

. . . .

Analogies are never perfect, but the Poles do have what we want. Consider the Poles: consider the price they have paid and paid and paid.

– Ray Smith
"Cape Breton is the Thought-Control Centre of Canada"

———

Fool
　　you *are* home
　　　　you were home
　　in the first place. . . .

– Miriam Waddington,
"Driving Home"

———

. . . What will be written in the full culture of occupation
Will come, presently, tomorrow,
From millions whose hands can turn these rocks
　　　　　　　into children.

– F. R. Scott,
"Laurentian Shield"

It came as a shock to me to discover that my country's literature was not just British literature imported or American literature with something missing, that instead it had a distinct tradition and shape of its own. The shock was partly exhilarating, partly depressing – I'll explore both reactions later – and partly a kind of outraged surprise: why hadn't I been told? Our writers, apparently, had been working within this tradition for some time; but what they'd been writing had often been confused with – or compared for put-down purposes with – the products of other traditions. Canadian writers have not been trying to write American or English literature and failing; they've been writing Canadian literature. The general invisibility of this fact suggests that what we need now is not so much a way of writing Canadian literature as a way of reading it.

As I've tried to make clear, Canadian literature is not equivalent with "Canadian Content." Boy wearing Mountie suit meets Rose Marie with a maple-leaf in her hair is more likely to be an American musical comedy than a Canadian novel. But there's no reason why boy can't meet girl in Canadian literature; Canadian literature does not exclude the universals, it just handles them in a characteristic way. It's not necessarily the "subject matter" – families, Indians, and so forth – that constitutes the Canadian signature, but the attitudes to that subject matter, and through the attitudes the kinds of images and the outcomes of stories. But you can't read that signature (nor decide whether the book that incorporates it is well or badly written) if you've been looking all along for a different name.

The question, then, is not whether boy should meet girl in Winnipeg or in New York; instead it is, What happens in Canadian literature when boy meets girl? And what sort of boy, and what sort of girl? If you've got this far, you may predict that when boy meets girl she gets cancer and he gets hit by a meteorite. . . .

That wasn't just a bad joke; it indicates the dangers of cliché writing once there's a defined tradition, and that in turn raises an important question: What do you do with a tradition once you discover you have one? The answers in terms of the Canadian tradition can get rather complicated, but I'll make two simple initial suggestions:

- If you're a writer, you need not discard the tradition, nor do you have to succumb to it. That is, you don't have to say, "The Canadian tradition is all about victims and failures, so I won't have anything to do with it"; nor need you decide that in order to be truly Canadian you have to give in and squash your hero under a tree. Instead, you can explore the tradition – which is not the same as merely reflecting it – and in the course of the exploration you may find some new ways of writing.
- If you're a reader, you can learn to read the products of the tradition *in terms of the tradition itself*. You don't knock Faulkner for not being Jane Austen, and those who do reveal nothing but their own obtuseness; the terms of reference are completely different. Recognizing your own tradition won't make you less critical; on the contrary, it ought to make you a better critic. (I'm not suggesting that you pretend bad writing is good, or fall into the trap of praising something just because it's Canadian.)

I'd like to explore these two areas – writing and reading – in a little more depth. I'll begin as usual with writing. There are two recent short stories which indicate one possible direction in which the tradition can be explored, as well as pulling together our central themes in some interesting ways. Their exploration consists of making explicit the experience of being a victim in a colonial culture – rendering it self-conscious as a literary theme.

The first story, by Ray Smith, is called "Cape Breton is the Thought-Control Centre of Canada." Using a form Smith terms "compiled fiction," it juxtaposes snatches of prose which follow three main threads: a dialogue between a married couple; a fantasy about the Americans invading Canada and the guerilla resistance movement which fights them; and the fictitious history of one Count Z., a Pole who is loath to cede Poland to either the Germans or the Russians. The married couple, when they are not lukewarmly discussing whether or not they love each other, are debating whether they should move to the States; the resistance movement material is done as movie and thriller cliché; and poor Count Z. gets cut down leading a cavalry charge in the war that ensues when he will not sell his country to either contender – after which the Germans and the Russians sit down at the bargaining table and divide Poland.

Smith's story is an illustration of what can result in literature when the Canada-as-collective-victim theme surfaces or becomes conscious, instead of remaining submerged as it is in much of our literature. Calvinism and Colonialism have always fed each other, and their interaction is circular: Calvinism gives rise to the "I am doomed" attitude, which fits into the Colonial "I am powerless" one. But in much of our earlier literature, the Calvinism is in the foreground, and the Colonialism, with all the feelings of cultural self-deprecation and insignificance that go with it, in the background. In Smith's story these positions are reversed. The story approaches the Colonial predicament from three different angles: the indistinctness and, finally, the *unreality* of the national situation viewed from the cozy domestic nest; the fantasy nature of possible resistance against imperialism (without an actual resistance movement, the individual's dreams of standing up to the "enemy" can remain only Walter Mitty dreams); and the spectacle of what happens, historically, to small nations caught between big ones when the former try to preserve their own identity. Poland is the place where the others fight it out. "Polish history is very simple in this way," Smith comments. "The Poles also are simple: they love Poland." Smith's story not only points the finger at "the enemy" (identified as America); it suggests too that resistance is absolutely necessary, though possibly futile and perhaps even ludicrous, as his parting joke indicates: "For Centennial Year, send President Johnson a gift: an American tourist's ear in a matchbox. Even better, don't bother with the postage."

The second story, by David Godfrey, is called "The Hard-Headed Collector," and it too uses the technique of intercut story lines. The main plot concerns the epic journey of seven men from West to East across a mythologized Canada, on their way to an important goal. They appear to be artists: singers, poets, carvers. One by one they are lured away from their quest by various temptations – material comforts such as food and sex, demands by other groups that they be leaders or priest-figures, calls to battle – or captured by hostile elements – one becomes a slave in a whorehouse to pay debts incurred there, another is tortured and castrated by the Town Fathers and discovers he likes it. Only one man makes it to the end of the journey, and it is there that we discover what the quest was about: the men were to have forged a magic axe, cut down a giant tree with it, and then presumably – since despite their diverse ethnic names they were all from the Queen Charlotte Islands – made a totem pole, symbol of unity, ancestry and identity. But the last survivor is too late: all the trees have either been ruined by flooding or turned into the produce of a lumberyard. He is given a menial job and dies shortly afterwards. A ship comes for his body, suggesting that he is a figure of heroic stature, like King Arthur, though a failed one.

This piece of myth-making is interspersed with scraps of documentary, from the *New York Times*, about an aggressive American capitalist of the rugged individualist school, the "hard-headed collector" of the title, who has used his stock-market and investment earnings to compile a valuable art collection. He is donating his collection to the United States, because "I couldn't do what I did in any other country." The art is to be put in a Washington museum. The money that bought it has been made from Canadian oil and uranium.

If we read the myth part of the story alone, it would appear that opposition to the artists and to their task comes only from elements within the society: the bourgeoisie who offer bread and security in return for being entertained, the credit-system whores who enslave through debt, the factionalism that makes battles, the religious fanatics who convert artistic vision to their own uses, the Town Fathers who are petty politicians and amputation experts. But when the "collector" sections are added the meaning shifts. The collector lives in the centre of the Empire but makes his money on its fringes; the ultimate end of his activities is to reduce both art and the environment to a commodity. "You have forsworn me," says the remaining artist to the manager of the lumberyard; to which the latter replies "Forsworn you, my ass. Terms is terms." The lumberyard is part of the Empire; it acknowledges only money; in fact, it exists to convert the environment into money, whereas the artists wish to convert it into art. At the centre of the Empire art is a thing to be gathered and exchanged, easily and without pain. On its fringes it is a thing that cannot even be produced. In the vain attempt much blood is spilled, but the country has been sold before its identity can be forged. Though elements within the society have co-operated against the full expression of that society, it is the "collector" and his like who have created the conditions for that co-operation.

Both these stories are firmly within the tradition we've been examining; but both break new ground in an important way. They are stories about failure and victimization; but they are naming real causes of victimization, not displacing the causes onto Fate or the Cosmos. And unlike most other books, they include political realities – the United States as an imperial master – among the causes of victimization which can be explored. As in Hubert Aquin's *Prochain Episode*, successful action against these causes can as yet be taken only in fantasies, or projected into the future: Smith's characters remain powerless and trapped, Godfrey's fail in their quest and die. But here, we feel, failure occurs not because the author's literary tradition demands a failure but because failure is consistent with the conditions depicted in the stories. A successful revolution in the present is not imaginable. And it's at points like these – when literature names situations we can recognize – that writer and reader connect in an area we can call real life: it's *our* situation that's being talked about (which is not to deny that readers of, say, MacLennan and Garner had the same feeling). A friend of mine has two phrases he falls back on when literature or reality get rough: "It's only a book" and "It's only my life." Sometimes the two can be used interchangeably.

I chose these two stories because they're short, they're experimental, and they deal with traditional Canadian themes in new ways. What is new about the approach is its consciousness, the making explicit of something that was hitherto implicit: Smith's analytical investigation of what it is to be a colony of the

American Empire, Godfrey's mythological dramatization of the same fact of life. There are other books that approach different areas of our tradition in an equally conscious way, and I've mentioned some of them (such as Cohen's *Beautiful Losers* and Blais's *A Season in the Life of Emmanuel*) elsewhere in this book. What such works suggest is that a writer does not have to repeat his tradition unaltered. He can explore it further, dig out all its implications; or he can play variations on it, even make departures from it which will gain their impact from their measurement against the basic ground of the main tradition.

————◁◦▷————

When I started thinking about whether or not anyone had attempted in poetry what Godfrey and Smith had done in prose – the mythologizing or analyzing of the country's predicament as a political victim – I found myself remembering a number of individual poems, but not very many books of poetry. Also, the tendency in English Canada has been to connect one's social protest not with the Canadian predicament specifically but with some other group or movement: the workers in the thirties, persecuted minority groups such as the Japanese uprooted during the war. English Canadians have identified themselves with Ban the Bombers, Communists, the F.L.Q., and so forth, but not often with each other – after all, the point of identifying with those other groups was at least partly to distinguish oneself from all the grey WASP Canadians you were afraid you might turn into.

But four books stand out: Dorothy Livesay's *Collected Poems* (especially "The Documentaries" and "The Thirties"), Milton Acorn's *I've Tasted My Blood*, bill bissett's *Nobody Owns th Earth*, and Dennis Lee's *Civil Elegies*. These are four extremely different poets, but all have two things in common: they connect individual oppression with group oppression and individual liberation with group liberation, and they connect social liberation with sexual liberation; or, to put it another way, social liberation means Nature no longer has to be dead or a monster. Especially in Acorn and Bissett, this liberation extends to a liberation of the language, which includes the use of four-letter words and, in Bissett, phonetic spelling. In the work of all four, liberation means roughly the same thing: the freedom to live a life which realizes to the full its available human possibilities, and to live that life by participating joyfully in one's "own" place. For Livesay and Acorn one's "own" place (in their poetry, at least) tends to be The World; for Bissett and Lee this place is emphatically Canada. Since the subject of this book is Canada I will concentrate on the two later poets, though anyone writing poems of social concern and action in this country must acknowledge a debt to the earlier ones.

The amazing thing about Bissett's book is that it juxtaposes visions of Edenic happiness and peace with angry political poems like "Th Canadian" and "Love of Life, th 49th Parallel," the latter being probably the most all-inclusive poem on American takeover to appear so far. And yet it isn't, finally, amazing: anger and the desire for change depend on the assumption that change will be for the better, that it is in fact possible to achieve not only individual but social freedom. The title, *Nobody Owns th Earth*, predicts a world that will be not "international" but post-national, in which people will live on the earth with love both for it and for each other, and some of the individual poems give us glimpses of this world. The angry "political" poems, however, recognize the fact that we do not yet live in this world, and if we assume too soon that the millennium has arrived we will simply end up as victims again, owned by people who do not even admit the possibility of a non-"owned" Earth. These Bissett identifies as "th Americans." A lot of the energy in the poems comes from the frustration experienced by someone who lives in the freedom of Position Four, communes with the mysticism of Position Five, but is forced to witness the effects of Position Two on himself and those around him. Like Blake, Bissett is a kind of social visionary, and for such a visionary there must always be Songs of Experience as well as Songs of Innocence. Paradise here and now is individual and sexual, Hell here and now is social and mechanical; but the potential for social redemption is present, as witness the strength of the image at the beginning of "Nobody Owns th Earth," in which "a whole peopul" is seen "moving / together."

Bissett can make images of the two poles of Hell and Paradise, but he isn't sure how we can get from one to the other. Dennis Lee's *Civil Elegies* contains the same two poles, Hell which is a condition of servitude, being "owned," and Paradise which would be a form of freedom; but instead of simply presenting the images Lee investigates them, and investigates also the process of transition, the choices that would have to be made before reaching the potential Paradise. One important difference between the two books is that Bissett places himself to some extent "outside" the society, as a rebel against "straight" Canada as well as the United States, and thus for him sexual freedom and ecstatic vision are possible; while Lee is "inside," he makes himself a representative of his society. He embodies its plight, and since domination by an empire involves both cultural castration and stunting of vision, he is blocked off to a greater extent from the sources of light.

Civil Elegies leads off with a quote from George Grant: "Man is by nature a political animal, and to know that citizenship is an impossibility is to be cut off from one of the highest forms of life." It is the impossibility, or near-impossibility of "citizenship" in Canada that the poem deals with, tracing the historical roots of the predicament and exposing its results. Because Canada was never claimed by and for the people who live there – there were, after all, foreign flags on those historic flagpoles – the citizens dwell in a kind of limbo, a state of unreal suspension. What must happen is a claiming, a "will to be" in this country. Lee does not make explicit which comes first, rebellion against the dominating Empire or the individual and group self-confidence (call it faith) required to sustain such a rebellion. But both, it appears, are necessary if we are not to live forever on "occupied soil."

Part of *Civil Elegies* is concerned with the relationship to the land, as are many of the poems in *Nobody Owns th Earth*. For both poets Nature is no longer a monster but a potential home; both protest the kind of attitude towards the land that results in its exploitation, men taking with their machines what there is to take. Both urge us to control our own space, physical as well as cultural. But that space must be controlled with love or it will be the control typical of a tyranny: there will not be that much difference between Canadian ownership and the absentee-landlord draining of the land we already live under. (Exploitation without representation wasn't good for Ireland either.) If choices destructive towards the land are made it doesn't much matter finally who makes them. But there is more chance of destructive choices being made by outsiders than by people who will have to endure the effects of these choices because they actually inhabit the country.

I'm not saying that all writing should be "experimental," or that all writing should be "political." But the fact that English Canadian writers are beginning to voice their own predicament consciously, as French Canadian writers have been doing for a decade, is worth mentioning. For both groups, this "voicing" is both an exploratory plunge into their own tradition and a departure from it; and for both groups the voicing would have been unimaginable twenty years ago.

———◆◇◆———

These then, are some of the directions writers are now moving in. What about readers? I said earlier that readers could learn to read the works of their tradition in terms of the tradition itself; and this act would seem to involve a double perspective or vision. Imagine a picture of a landscape in which everything is dark grey – sky, lake, shore – except for a few points of light – a red flower, or a small fire, or a human figure. (Except for the colour scheme – blue, green and white are preferred to dark grey – this could in fact be a description of an actual Canadian painting, since many of them employ the same composition.) You can look at the picture with two attitudes. You can decide that the grey landscape is so large and overpowering that the points of light are totally dominated by it, rendered insignificant. Or you can see the points of light in contrast to their surroundings: their dark background sets them off and gives them meaning in a way that a bright one would not.

The tone of Canadian literature as a whole is, of course, the dark background: a reader must face the fact that Canadian literature is undeniably sombre and negative, and that this to a large extent is both a reflection and a chosen definition of the national sensibility. (That is, the artist takes his colouring from his environment, though he may intensify it by adding a little murk of his own.) But in that literature there are elements which, although they are rooted in this negativity, transcend it – the collective hero, the halting but authentic breakthroughs made by characters who are almost hopelessly trapped, the moments of affirmation that neither deny the negative ground nor succumb to it. These elements are not numerous, but they gain their significance from their very scarcity: thus, in Canadian literature, a character who does much more than survive stands out almost as an anomaly, whereas in other literatures (those in which European Princes are common, for instance) his presence would be unremarkable.

I said at the beginning of this chapter that when I discovered the shape of the national tradition I was depressed, and it's obvious why: it's a fairly tough tradition to be saddled with, to have to come to terms with. But I was exhilarated too: having bleak ground under your feet is better than having no ground at all. Any map is better than no map as long as it is accurate, and knowing your starting points and your frame of reference is better than being suspended in a void. A tradition doesn't necessarily exist to bury you: it can also be used as material for new departures.

The title of this chapter comes from a poem by Margaret Avison, which begins:

Nobody stuffs the world in at your eyes.
The optic heart must venture: a jail-break
and re-creation . . .

What these three lines suggest is that in none of our acts – even the act of looking – are we passive. Even the things we look at demand our participation, and our commitment: if this participation and commitment are given, what can result is a "jail-break," an escape from our old habits of looking at things, and a "re-creation," a new way of seeing, experiencing and imaging – or imagining – which we ourselves have helped to shape.

I'll leave you with two questions which someone asked me while reading the manuscript of this book:

Have we survived?
If so, what happens *after* Survival?

Short List:

BISSETT, bill, *Nobody Owns th Earth*; AN, $2.50.
LEE, Dennis, *Civil Elegies*; AN, $2.50.

Long List:

ACORN, Milton, *I've Tasted My Blood*; R.
AQUIN, Hubert, *Prochain Episode*; NCL.
AVISON, Margaret, "Snow," *Winter Sun*; UTP. Also G&B.
BISSETT, bill, *Nobody Owns th Earth*; AN.
BLAIS, Marie-Claire, *A Season in the Life of Emmanuel*; Grosset's Universal Library.
COHEN, Leonard, *Beautiful Losers*; Bantam.
GODFREY, Dave, "The Hard-Headed Collector," *Death Goes Better with Coca-Cola*; Press Porcépic. Also *Great Canadian Short Stories* (ed. Lucas); Dell.
LEE, Dennis, *Civil Elegies*; AN.
LIVESAY, Dorothy, *Collected Poems*; R.
SMITH, Ray, "Cape Breton is the Thought-Control Centre of Canada," *Cape Breton is the Thought-Control Centre of Canada*; AN.

Sources of Epigraphs

Introductory

Saint-Denys-Garneau, "The Body of This Death," translated by
John Glassco; in *French Canadian Poetry in Translation*,
(ed. Glassco). OUP.

Margaret Avison, "The Agnes Cleves Papers," *Winter Sun*;
UTP, OP.

Preface

Brian Moore, *The Luck of Ginger Coffey*; NCL, p. 214.

Germaine Warkentin, "An Image In A Mirror," *Alphabet*, No. 8.

George Grant, *Technology and Empire*; AN, p. 68.

Northrop Frye, *The Bush Garden*; AN, p. 220.

Margaret Avison, "Not the Sweet Cicely of Gerardes Herball,"
Winter Sun; UTP, OP.

Chapter One

John Newlove, "If You Can," *Moving In Alone*; Contact Press, OP.

Al Purdy, "Autumn," *Wild Grape Wine*; M&S.

Russell Marois, *The Telephone Pole*; AN, p. 14.

John Newlove, "Like a Canadian," *Black Night Window*; M&S.

D. G. Jones, "Beating the Bushes: Christmas 1963," *Phrases
from Orpheus*; OUP.

Chapter Two

Northrop Frye, *The Bush Garden*; AN, p. 225.

E. J. Pratt, *Towards the Last Spike*; Macmillan. Also *Selected
Poems*; Macmillan.

Alice Munro, *Lives of Girls and Women*; R, p. 87.

Douglas LePan, "Coureurs de Bois," *The Book of Canadian
Poetry* (ed. A. J. M. Smith); Gage.

D. G. Jones, "Soliloquy to Absent Friends," *The Sun Is Axeman*; UTP.

George Grant, *Technology and Empire*; AN, p. 24.

Chapter Three

Ernest Thompson Seton, "Redruff," *Wild Animals I Have Known*; Schocken Books, p. 317.

John Newlove, "The Well-Travelled Roadway," *Moving In Alone*; Contact Press, OP.

Alden Nowlan, "A Night Hawk Fell With a Sound Like a Shudder," *Under The Ice*; R, OP.

Stuart MacKinnon, "On the Way to the Vivarium," *Skydeck*; Oberon. (Also *The Broken Ark*, ed. Ondaatje, Oberon.)

Al Purdy, "The Sculptors," *North of Summer*; M&S. (Also *Selected Poems*, M&S.)

Graeme Gibson, *Five Legs*; AN, p. 112.

Chapter Four

Charles Mair, *Tecumseh*, excerpt in *The Book of Canadian Poetry* (ed. A. J. M. Smith); Gage.

E. J. Pratt, *Brébeuf and His Brethren*; Macmillan. (Also *Selected Poems*, Macmillan.)

James Reaney, "The Canadian Poet's Predicament," in *Masks of Poetry* (ed. A. J. M. Smith); NCL, p. 119.

A. M. Klein, "Indian Reservation: Caughnawaga," *The Rocking Chair*; R.

George Grant, *Technology and Empire*; AN, p. 17.

Leonard Cohen, *Beautiful Losers*; Bantam, p. 5.

Chapter Five

Al Purdy, "The North West Passage," *Wild Grape Wine*; M&S.

George Bowering, "the oil," *Rocky Mountain Foot*; M&S.

Dennis Lee, *Civil Elegies*; AN.

Al Purdy, "The Country North of Belleville," *The Cariboo Horses*; M&S.

Gwen MacEwen, *Terror and Erebus*; C.B.C play, not in print.

Chapter Six

Elizabeth Brewster, "Local Graveyard," *Passage of Summer*; R.

Dorothy Roberts, "Cold," *Dazzle*; R, OP.

Hugh MacLennan, *Each Man's Son*; Macmillan, p. 64.

Margaret Laurence, *A Bird in the House*; NCL, p. 92.

Tom Wayman, "Opening the Family," *Mindscapes*; AN.

Chapter Seven

John Marlyn, *Under the Ribs of Death*; NCL, p. 24.

George Jonas, "Five More Lines," *The Absolute Smile*; AN, OP.

Walter Bauer, "Emigrants" (translated by Henry Beissel), *Volvox*; Sono Nis.

Alden Nowlan, "Alex Duncan," *Under the Ice*; R, OP.

Chapter Eight

Leonard Cohen, "A Migrating Dialogue," *Selected Poems*; M&S.

Dennis Lee, *Civil Elegies*; AN.

John Newlove, "Crazy Riel," *Black Night Window*; M&S.

George Grant, *Technology and Empire*; AN, p. 67.

Chapter Nine

Anne Hébert, "Manor Life" (translated by F. R. Scott), *The Poetry of French Canada in Translation*; OUP.

A. M. Klein, "Portrait of the Poet as Landscape," *The Rocking Chair*; R. (also *Poets Between the Wars* ed. Wilson; NCL).

James Reaney, "The Upper Canadian," *Selected Poems*; N.

Elizabeth Brewster, "Gold Man," *Sunrise North*; Clarke Irwin.

Chapter Ten
Warren Tallman, "Wolf in the Snow," *Contexts of Canadian Criticism*; UTP.
Phyllis Webb, "Beachcomber," *Selected Poems*; Talonbooks.
James Reaney, *One-Man Masque*; *The Killdeer and Other Plays*; Macmillan.
Sheila Watson, *The Double Hook*; NCL, p. 49.
Anne Wilkinson, "The Pressure of Night," *The Hangman Ties The Holly*; Macmillan. OP.
Jay Macpherson, "The Caverned Woman," *The Boatman*; OUP.

Chapter Eleven
Gabrielle Roy, *The Tin Flute*; NCL, p. 256.
Saint-Denys-Garneau, "Spectacle of the Dance," (translated by F. R. Scott), *French Canadian Poetry in Translation*; OUP.
Yves Préfontaine, "Country to Let," (translated by G. V. Downes), *French Canadian Poetry in Translation*; OUP.
Roch Carrier, *La Guerre, Yes Sir!*; AN, p. 41.
Hubert Aquin, *Prochain Episode*; NCL, p. 21.
Marie-Claire Blais, *A Season in the Life of Emmanuel*; Grosset's Universal Library, p. 79.

Chapter Twelve
Patrick Anderson, "Poem on Canada," excerpt in *The Blasted Pine* (ed. F. R. Scott and A. J. M. Smith); Macmillan. Also *The Penguin Book of Canadian Verse*, (ed. Gustafson; 1958 edition); Penguin.
Dennis Lee, *Civil Elegies*; AN.
Ray Smith, "Cape Breton is the Thought-Control Centre of Canada," *Cape Breton is the Thought-Control Centre of Canada*; AN.
Miriam Waddington, "Driving Home," *Say Yes*; OUP.
F. R. Scott, "Laurentian Shield," *Poets Between the Wars* (ed. Milton Wilson); NCL.

Authors' Index

Margaret Atwood was born in 1939 in Ottawa and grew up in Quebec, northern Ontario and Toronto.

She is the author of more than fifty volumes of poetry, fiction, and nonfiction. Her novels include *The Edible Woman* (1970), *The Handmaid's Tale* (1985), *The Robber Bride* (1994), *Alias Grace* (1996), *The Blind Assassin*, *Oryx and Crake* and *The Year of the Flood*. Her most recent works of nonfiction are *Payback: Debt and the Shadow Side of Wealth*, on which the recent film, *Payback*, is based, and *In Other Worlds: SF and the Human Imagination*. Her most recent children's book is *Wandering Wenda and Widow Wallop's Wunderground Washery*. Ms. Atwood's work has been published in more than forty languages; a number of her titles have been adapted for theatre, opera, television and film. She is the recipient of numerous awards.

Margaret Atwood lives in Toronto with writer Graeme Gibson. They are the Joint Honorary Presidents of the Rare Bird Society of Birdlife International. Ms. Atwood is also a Vice President of International PEN.